# Fun Halloween Riddles & Trick Questions for Kids and Family

## 300 Riddles and Brain Teasers that Kids and Family Will Enjoy!

### With Fun Illustrations

**Riddleland**

# Table of Contents

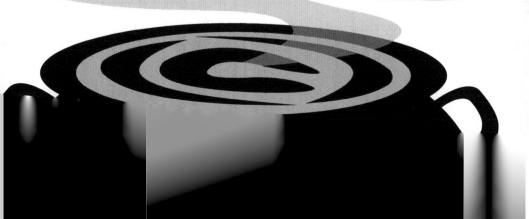

## bonus book

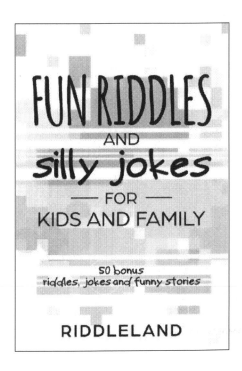

FUN RIDDLES
AND
silly jokes
— FOR —
KIDS AND FAMILY

50 bonus
riddles, jokes and funny stories

RIDDLELAND

SCAN ME

Thank you for buying this book. As a token of our appreciation, we would like to offer a special bonus - a collection of 50 original jokes, riddles and funny stories

# Introduction

## "Magic is really very simple. All you've got to do is want something and then let yourself have it."
### ~ Aggie Cromwell

We would like to personally thank you for purchasing this book. **Fun Halloween Riddles and Trick Questions for Kids and Family!** book is a collection of 300 fun brain teasers and riddles of easy to hard difficulty.

These brain teasers will challenge children and parents to stretch their minds. They also have many other benefits such as:

•  **Bonding** – These riddles are an excellent way for parents and children to complete together while creating some fun memories.

•  **Confidence Building** - Our brain benders provide children an opportunity to think for themselves or collaborate with parents, siblings, or friends; practice their problem solving skills, and experience the joy of success or the challenge of making mistakes - all in a safe environment.

- **Improve Vocabulary** – Riddles may be written using a broad vocabulary range. Children will be challenged to learn and understand new words.

- **Better reading comprehension** – Although many children are able to read at a young age, not all are able to understand the context of the words they are reading. The desire to solve a riddle will motivate children to further develop their reading comprehension

- **Sense of humor** – Funny creative riddles can help children develop their sense of humor while getting their brains working.

# Chapter 1

# Spooky Riddles

"May you scare more and get scared less on this Halloween"

~ Unknown

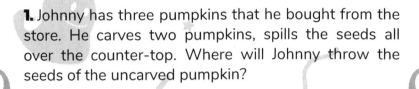

**1.** Johnny has three pumpkins that he bought from the store. He carves two pumpkins, spills the seeds all over the counter-top. Where will Johnny throw the seeds of the uncarved pumpkin?

_____

**2.** Jane makes three pumpkin pies in the oven. She places one on the windowsill to cool. How many does she have left on the counter?

_____

**3.** I am waxy and sweet. I am a variety of colors, and I am named after a starchy vegetable, but I am candy. You try to eat just one, but it turns into a whole bag.

**What am I?**

_____

**4.** You could see me before, but you can't see me now. I used to be alive. If you try to touch me, your hand will pass right through. Wear a bedsheet, and you'll look just like me.

**What am I?**

_____

**5.** What is the title of a writer who writes but does not take credit for what is written? The name sounds haunting, but the writer is usually alive and well.

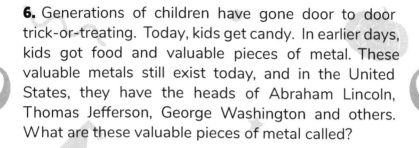

## Chapter 1 - Questions

**6.** Generations of children have gone door to door trick-or-treating. Today, kids get candy. In earlier days, kids got food and valuable pieces of metal. These valuable metals still exist today, and in the United States, they have the heads of Abraham Lincoln, Thomas Jefferson, George Washington and others. What are these valuable pieces of metal called?

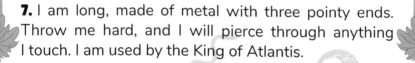

**7.** I am long, made of metal with three pointy ends. Throw me hard, and I will pierce through anything I touch. I am used by the King of Atlantis.

**What am I?**

**8.** I walk around terrorizing the town's people. I am big and scary with bolts in my neck, but I was created by a person.

**Who am I?**

**9.** I am used to make non-permanent markings to disguise your face. I come in many different colors.

**What am I?**

**10.** I am brown on the outside, have coconut on the inside, but I am not found on a tree. I can be found in a candy package with a twin.

**What am I?**

**Chapter 1 - Questions**

**11.** I am a witch's male counterpart. I can still cast spells like the best of them.

**What am I?**

**12.** This structure always looks angry on Halloween with its sinister face because it is feeling hollow inside after getting carved out.

**What is it?**

**13.** Even though it may feature a zombie, a haunted scarecrow, or a giant moth instead of me personally, these haunting stories all feature my name. I am the main character in many of these scary tales.

**What kind of tales are these?**

**Chapter 1 - Questions**

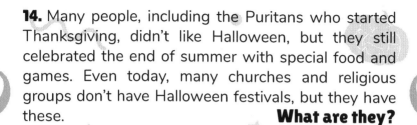

**14.** Many people, including the Puritans who started Thanksgiving, didn't like Halloween, but they still celebrated the end of summer with special food and games. Even today, many churches and religious groups don't have Halloween festivals, but they have these. **What are they?**

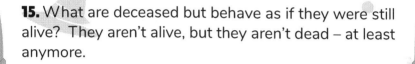

**15.** What are deceased but behave as if they were still alive? They aren't alive, but they aren't dead – at least anymore.

**16.** I have the ability to drive through a vampire's heart, stopping them dead in their tracks.

**What am I?**

**17.** People used to wear costumes and light bonfires to keep me away. Some things go bump in the night; I am known for going, "Boo!"

**What am I?**

**18.** When you have ghosts who are out of control, who you gonna call? "Wink"

**Chapter 1 - Questions**

**19.** Typically depicted as a female, casting spells and riding by night on a household cleaning item.

**What is she?**

**20.** Witches have to store their brooms, and, instead of a garage, they typically use a broom closet. If two of the witch's brooms are stored in the same broom closet, what is their relationship to each other?

---

**21.** I am the most precious dish on this holiday; I carry many treats to give out to the kids on Halloween.

**What am I?**

**22.** When a witch rides in the rain, her hair does not get wet.

**Why is this?**

# Halloween Fun Facts

Did you know that the White House, is said to be haunted by the ghost of Abraham Lincoln? His ghost has been spotted by many famous people at the White House, including Lady Eleanor Roosevelt and Sir Winston Churchill.

**23.** You can use me to climb to a higher place step by step. Walk under me, and I will bring you bad luck.

**What am I?**

**Chapter 1 - Questions**

**24.** I am large and white. I can be cold or warm. You use me when you go to sleep. Cut eye holes in me and put me over someone, and they will look like a ghost.

**What am I?**

**25.** I am small, and I have pointy ears. Sometimes I am good, and sometimes, I am evil. Bow and arrows are my weapon of choice.

**What am I?**

**26.** I may look like an innocent feline with my dark fur, but if you walk by me, i will bring you bad luck (or so I am told).

**What am I?**

## Chapter 1 - Questions

**27.** I sleep all day and drink the substance of life that flows through everyone all night. I hate garlic. If I am outside on a sunny day, I will waste away.

**What am I?**

**28.** You put me on your food to add taste. Don't confuse me with sugar because I look the same. Spill me, and I will bring you bad luck.

**What am I?**

**29.** I am the Roman Catholic leader who designated November 1 as All Saints Day. Ironically, this created Hallowed Evening which was shorted to Hallowed Eve and then to Halloween, one last chance for evil to thrive before the saints were celebrated. My name rhymes with "hope". **Who am I?**

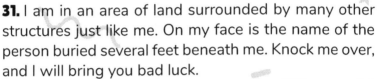

**30.** As you feel me pumping faster, know that you are getting more frightened.

**What am I?**

**31.** I am in an area of land surrounded by many other structures just like me. On my face is the name of the person buried several feet beneath me. Knock me over, and I will bring you bad luck.

**What am I?**

**32.** Based on my name you would think I was hungry; however, I would rather bang on pots and pans rather than do any cooking.

**What am I?**

**33.** Witches typically ride broomsticks made of wood and me. I am the one who broke the camel's back.

**What am I?**

**34.** I am a good luck piece on a necklace; I also cast a spell. I am associated with good manners; lovers use me to woo each other.

**What am I?**

**35.** Reading at night can help you fall asleep, but after I read these, I'm too afraid to go to sleep.

**What am I reading?**

**36.** The evil witch likes to turn handsome princes into me when they refuse to marry her. Now if only I can get a princess to kiss me before I croak.

**What am I?**

**37.** This vehicle is rather silly. It has no wheels or seats. Just a pole to climb upon to whisk you off your feet.

**What is it?**

**38.** I am wrapped in bandages, but I don't have open wounds. I may be thousands of years old but can often still move. I stalk through the night slowly.

**What am I?**

**39.** I ride a horse, and I wear a special hat. I love the old Wild West and to round up things with my rope.

**What am I?**

**40.** If you see me in the cemetery, it is better to be above the grave, than in it. I may not harm you while you're living, but you don't want me around if you're in the grave. I am so evil that I will not feed on you unless you are dead. That is why the graveyard is my favorite place.

**Who am I?**

**41.** I am a fruit, but I am also a candy. They put me on a stick because I am quite messy.

**What am I?**

# Halloween Fun Facts

Do you know that some people are afraid of Halloween? Their fear is called Samhainophobia!

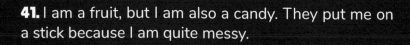

**42.** I may be a simple squash plant for most of the year, but during this season, I am the symbol that is most closely associated with Halloween.

**What am I?**

**Chapter 1 - Questions**

**43.** You look at me to see yourself. When you want to make sure you look good, you look into me. Break me, and I will bring you bad luck.

**What am I?**

**44.** How do you keep a witch from leaving her cave?

**45.** When you wear me, no one knows who you are. I can be scary, cute, fun, or anything you can imagine.

**What am I?**

## Chapter 1 - Questions

**46.** I was bitten in the night by a mysterious furry creature. Now, when the moon is full, I also become this creature.

**What am I?**

**47.** I fly higher than a bat. I am the only dinosaur with the name terror in it. I have a long face and a long neck, a short tail, and giant wings.

**Who am I?**

**48.** What is the essential tool needed to groom a werewolf?

**Chapter 1** - Questions

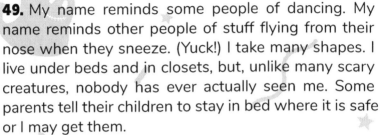

**49.** My name reminds some people of dancing. My name reminds other people of stuff flying from their nose when they sneeze. (Yuck!) I take many shapes. I live under beds and in closets, but, unlike many scary creatures, nobody has ever actually seen me. Some parents tell their children to stay in bed where it is safe or I may get them.

**Who am I?**

**50.** These people who started Halloween did not sell ticks, but their name sure sounds like they did. What was this group of people called? (Hint: They also gave us Leprechauns and four-leaf clovers; do you feel lucky?)

**51.** I love riding horses. I am not prim and proper. I love dirt and riding through the night, just like my male friends.

**What am I?**

**52.** If I don't have eggs for your trick, I will have this paper instead to throw all around your house.

**What paper is it?**

**53.** If you invite a vampire over to your house, what dish do you need to make sure you serve?

**54.** I am everyone's favorite pie made from the symbol most associated with Halloween.

**What am I?**

**55.** I am large and scary. If you see me, you will run. I don't have a specific look, but I will scare the pants off anybody because I am scary and evil. I will scream at you and make you go the other way.

**What am I?**

**56.** It slithers through the night. It is long and scary. If you don't bother it, it won't bother you.

**What is it?**

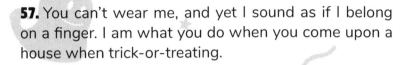

## Chapter 1 - Questions

**57.** You can't wear me, and yet I sound as if I belong on a finger. I am what you do when you come upon a house when trick-or-treating.

**What am I?**

**58.** I am the ghost of the sixteenth President. Although I was born in Illinois, I haunt the White House to this day. I am a true American spirit.

**Who am I?**

**59.** I sail on the water carrying those who pillage and plunder as they go.

**What am I?**

**60.** Ding Dong! Ding Dong! This is the sound you hear coming from my heart as you look at me up high. The sound can be heard for miles and I will let you know when there is a special occasion happening as I sing my praises throughout the sky.

**What am I?**

**61.** I am a food with lots of eyes. When the Irish could not grow me in Ireland one year, they came to the United States, bringing their Halloween customs with them. I am greatly responsible for Halloween as it is today.

**What am I?**

**62.** Don't come inside the doors. I may look like a home, but I am filled with ghosts, goblins, and ghouls.

**What am I?**

**63.** A woman is walking at night and looking down. Suddenly she looks to the left and sees a witch flying next to her. Why didn't she see the witch's shadow when she was looking down?

**64.** I come to your door. I want some good candy. Give it to me, or I have some eggs handy.

**Who am I?**

## Chapter 1 - Questions

**65.** Kids love Halloween, but I am the delicious treat that they love the most. If you don't have me when they walk up to your door, expect trouble.

**What am I?**

**66.** I am a season and I bring a chill to the air. The once green tree leaves are now brown and falling with despair. You love me because I am the season of dressing up and getting candy.

**What season am I?**

**67.** I am the symbol of Pomona, the Roman Goddess of fruit - a harvest goddess. People bob for me at Halloween

**What am I?**

**68.** Halloween is the second biggest holiday in terms of money spent, second only to me. If you play too many tricks on people at Halloween, you may not get a toy when I come around.

**What holiday am I?**

**69.** Linus of "Peanuts" would sit in the pumpkin patch each Halloween waiting for me. The other kids thought he was crazy, but every Halloween he would wait – and he would go to sleep before I came.

**Who am I?**

**70.** I live in the bell tower. I may look scary, but don't judge me until you see me.

**Who am I?**

---

# Halloween Fun Facts

Do you know what these are: All Hallows' Eve; Witches Night; Lamswool; Snap-Apple Night; Samhain; San-Apple Night; Nutcrack Night; and Summer's End? They're all other names for Halloween!

**71.** I'm loud and booming, a storm's a brewing. Sometimes my noise causes fear, if I'm too scary, cover your ears.

**What am I?**

**72.** I am the weapon of choice carried by death himself.

**What am I?**

**73.** I am a date that invokes terror, I fall near the end of the week and the middle of the month.

**What date am I?**

## Chapter 1 - Questions

**74.** I am a common household cleaning item, but for some, I am their mode of transportation.

### What am I?

**75.** I am what many pirates use to leave a ship. Usually not by their choice.

### What am I?

**76.** I am something a pumpkin needs when it gets an injury.

### What am I?

**77.** Halloween is the word. Now spell that without the letter L.

**78.** You have five mini pumpkins in a basket. You want to divide them evenly among five kids but still leave one in the basket.

### How will you do this?

**79.** When does Halloween happen after Christmas but before Thanksgiving?

**Chapter 1** - Questions

**80.** I have already died, but I still walk the earth. I enjoy eating the brains of my many victims.

**What am I?**

**81.** I create my own web, but I don't mean the Internet. I have more legs than you, but am much smaller ; even so, I can make grownups scream in terror.

**What am I?**

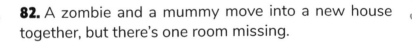

**82.** A zombie and a mummy move into a new house together, but there's one room missing.

**Which room is it?**

## Chapter 1 - Questions

**83.** The headless horseman comes into town with a matching outfit. His pants are brown, his jacket in brown and his shoes are brown.

### What color is his hat?

**84.** You have a match and three candles that you will use for your jack-o-lanterns. You have a tall candle, a medium sized candle and a short candle. Which one should you light first in order to be able to light all of the candles?

**85.** For those who are no longer living, for those who are in the grave. I am a stone that gives you people's names and how long they lived.

### What am I?

**86.** I am a red substance found in everyone. I rush around the body giving it life. If you see me outside of the body, it will make you scream.

### What am I?

**87.** For Halloween, Johnny buys four pumpkins, including an orange one. He gets a yellow one, a green one and a red one.

### What color is the fourth pumpkin?

**Chapter 1** - Questions

**88.** Argh! I may only have one eye. If you cross me and make me angry, I will make you walk the plank.

**What am I?**

**89.** I am a structure made of bones, and I am inside all of you. But if you see me by myself, I will scare the pants off you.

**What am I?**

**90.** If you have 20 candies from trick or treating and you drop your whole basket, how many do you have left?

## Chapter 1 - Questions

**91.** What is a witch's wicked laugh called when she is about to cause some terror to people in the village?

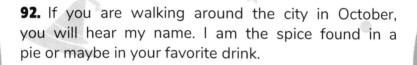

**92.** If you are walking around the city in October, you will hear my name. I am the spice found in a pie or maybe in your favorite drink.

**What am I?**

**93.** I sit upon a wire and watch people walking by. I have black feathers and a pointed beak. It's you I'd like to stalk.

**What am I?**

**94.** I bring brightness to a Jack-o-lantern. I am taller when I am young and shrink quickly as I work and get old.

**What am I?**

**95.** I am cold but I can cause severe burns. I can melt, but I don't turn into a liquid. I create smoke, but I also make things freeze.

**What am I?**

**Chapter 1** - Questions

**96.** A pirate must be very careful when taking care of an itch because I am sharp and have replaced their missing hand.

**What am I?**

**97.** If a group of zombies are involved in a crash, where would you bury the survivors?

**98.** A witch has two broomsticks. She breaks one but still has a spare. When she breaks the other one, she buys three to replace them. Eventually, she breaks one of the new ones she buys. How many broomsticks does she have left?

## Chapter 1 - Questions

**99.** When a pirate wears me, you cannot tell what color their hair is.

**What am I?**

**100.** What is the most recognizable way to distinguish different types of monsters? It is the first thing you hear from them.

**What is this?**

**101.** People used to leave me on the road to show their loved ones how to get back to the spirit world. Don't make light of my job; that's my job.

**What am I?**

**Chapter 1 - Questions**

**102.** This awful future will be mine if my path is crossed by a dark feline. What happens?

**103.** There are a group of witches racing on their broomsticks. If the witch in third place passes the witch in second place, what place is she in now?

**104.** Imagine you are in a room full of ghosts. What is the best way to escape the horror?

**105.** I am clear; you can see through me. Yet, if you touch me, you are covered with me. Come, bob for apples in me.

**What am I?**

**106.** This may be true, or it may be a myth, but in a movie, when a person gets a major spook, their hair often changes to a lighter color. What color are we talking about here?

---

# Halloween Fun Facts

Do you know how many Jack 'O Lanterns have been lit all at the same time? The record stands at 30,128. This was in Boston, Massachusetts.

---

**107.** I was minding my own business and had just started walking up the stairs when suddenly, something jumped out and startled me! I fell off the stairs, but did not receive any injuries.

**How is this possible?**

**Chapter 1 - Questions**

**108.** I am the symbol of evil with my red skin, pointed tail, and evil grin.

**Who am I?**

**109.** I am so knowledgeable; I am so smart. I can create anything using my mind and hands, but I choose to use my knowledge for wrongdoing.

**Who am I?**

**110.** I am a circular decoration hung on a door mostly found during Christmas. But there is a spookier version of me for Halloween.

**What am I?**

## Chapter 1 - Answers

1. Nowhere -this pumpkin isn't carved so the seeds are still inside

2. None on the counter, one on the windowsill and two in the oven.

3. Candy Corn.

4. Ghost

5. Ghostwriter

6. Coins (Abraham Lincoln is on the penny; Thomas Jefferson is on the nickel; George Washington is on the quarter)

7. Trident

8. Frankenstein's monster

9. Face paint

10. Almond Joy candy.

11. Warlock

12. Jack-O-Lantern

13. Ghost tales/ghost stories

14. Harvest Parties

15. The undead

16. Wooden stake

17. Ghost

18. Ghostbusters

19. A Witch

20. Broom-mates

21. Candy bowl.

22. She is wearing a pointy hat.

23. Ladder

24. A bedsheet.

25. An elf

26. Black cat

27. Vampire

28. Salt

29. Pope; Pope Gregory III to be exact

30. Heart

31. Gravestone

32. A goblin

33. Straw

34. Charm

35. Scary stories

36. Frog

37. A broomstick

38. Mummy

39. Cowboy

40. Ghoul

41. Candy apple or toffee apple

42. Pumpkin

43. Mirror

44. By breaking her broomstick

45. Halloween Costume

46. Werewolf

47. Terror-dactyl (Pterodactyl)

48. Comb

49. The Boogie Man

50. Celtic

51. Cowgirl

52. Toilet paper

53. Blood soup

54. Pumpkin pie

55. Monster

## Chapter 1 - Answers

| | | | |
|---|---|---|---|
| 56. | Snake | 72. | Sickle |
| 57. | Ring | 73. | Friday the 13th |
| 58. | Abraham Lincoln | 74. | Broom |
| 59. | Pirate ship | 75. | The plank |
| 60. | Bell Tower | 76. | Pumpkin patch |
| 61. | Potato | 77. | T-H-A-T |
| 62. | Haunted house | 78. | Give the fifth kid the pumpkin while the pumpkin is still in the basket. |
| 63. | Because it is night time | | |
| 64. | Trick of treater | 79. | In the dictionary. |
| 65. | Candy | 80. | Zombie |
| 66. | Fall or autumn | 81. | Spider |
| 67. | Apple | 82. | The living room |
| 68. | Christmas | 83. | He has no hat. He is the Headless horseman |
| 69. | The Great Pumpkin | | |
| 70. | Quasi Modo (The Hunchback of Notre Dame) | 84. | The match |
| 71. | Thunder | 85. | Gravestone |
| 86. | Blood | 99. | Bandana |
| 87. | Orange | 100. | Their roars |
| 88. | Pirate | 101. | Lantern |
| 89. | Skeleton | 102. | Bad luck |
| 90. | You still have 20, just on the floor. | 103. | Second |
| | | 104. | Stop imagining |
| 91. | Cackle | 105. | Water |
| 92. | Pumpkin Spice | 106. | White |
| 93. | A crow | 107. | I fell off only one or two steps because I just started walking up the stairs |
| 94. | Candle | | |
| 95. | Dry Ice | | |
| 96. | Hook | 108. | The devil |
| 97. | All zombies are dead. So you won't have to bury survivors | 109. | Evil Scientist |
| | | 110. | Wreath |
| 98. | Five. She still has the broken ones | | |

# Chapter 2

# Terrifying Riddles

"Don't scare ghosts too much, you little monster, otherwise, they will not come next year!"

~ Unknown

**Chapter 2 - Questions**

**1.** What is more evil than the devil, something you won't miss if you lose it, will be poor if you have it and will starve if you eat it?

_____

**2.** What is a skeleton's favorite instrument?

_____

**3.** The werewolf lives in a two-story house, including a basement. He decorates the walls of the main floor in red and wants to keep the house uniform. So, what color should he paint the walls upstairs?

_____

**4.** How much heavier is a 150-pound vampire than a 150-pound werewolf?

_____

**5.** How do you turn a ghost into a proper host?

**6.** I am filled with people, but nobody talks. I am filled with names, but nobody will answer to them. All you see is a bunch of rocks or stones for that matter.

**What am I?**

**7.** I am a mixture of multiple things. I can heal someone when they are sick or make someone ill when they are well. I can change your thoughts and I can put you to sleep. Drink me carefully and there could be many benefits that you reap.

**What am I?**

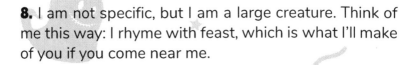

## Chapter 2 - Questions

**8.** I am not specific, but I am a large creature. Think of me this way: I rhyme with feast, which is what I'll make of you if you come near me.

**What am I?**

_____

**9.** If a vampire were to make a withdrawal, this is where he would go. It is filled to the brim with his favorite substance.

**What is it?**

_____

**10.** I protect the people I hide and the stones that exist inside of me from those who may wish to do harm.

**What am I?**

_____

**11.** In my regular state, I am a type of vegetable with a pungent aroma. I am rarely eaten alone. When you show me to a Vampire, they run away.

**What am I?**

_____

**12.** I am on full display for all to see. You walk by me in a front yard, you will see my glimmer, and I will look scary.

**What am I?**

**Chapter 2** - Questions

**13.** Witches can hold this without using their hands.

**What is it?**

---

**14.** What noise do werewolves make when they hunt for their prey?

**15.** Cold and creaky, leaking walls. Far away from castle halls. Tell me, criminal, before it's too late -what did you do to earn this fate?

**Where are you?**

**Chapter 2** - Questions

**16.** You know me as Halloween, but I am called something else in Spanish.

**What am I called?**

**17.** I am a large pot, and I am used for cooking, however, when people hear of me, they think of witchcraft and potions.

**What am I?**

**18.** A vampire just finished drinking the blood of one hundred people. When he tries to go through a metal detector, it beeps excessively.

**Why is that?**

**19.** I am depicted as a male, and I have magical powers. Boys go to magic school to be my apprentice.

**Who am I?**

**20.** I am edible and people love to eat me for breakfast. Kids will use me for mischievous acts when they don't get what they want while trick-or-treating.

**What am I?**

**21.** I occur at the beginning of night, and at the end of Halloween.

### What am I?

**22.** A witch, a ghost and a bat fly off the roof of a haunted house at the same time.

### Who will reach the ground first

**23.** Frankenstein's monster is eight feet tall and four feet wide. While walking through a closed doorway that is 10 feet tall and five feet wide, he gets blocked.

### How is that?

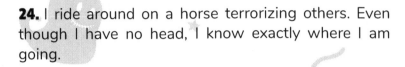

**Chapter 2 - Questions**

**24.** I ride around on a horse terrorizing others. Even though I have no head, I know exactly where I am going.

**Who am I?**

**25.** I have eye-sockets, but I cannot see. I used to be able to think, but now I am empty. I have a mouth but cannot eat. I am inside of you too, just hidden.

**What am I?**

**26.** If you are looking for me, I will be inside my box, sleeping tight so I can have my blood later. I am a vampire, but what am I sleeping in?

**27.** I am made of a common, everyday starchy vegetable. My walls are stacked high and I have multiple pathways. Lose your way and you will get lost inside of me for hours.

**What am I?**

**28.** Three little girls have a total of ten candy bars between them. The first girl gives the second girl two candy bars. The second girl decides she does not like one of them and gives it back to the first girl. She then gives three of her candy bars to the third girl, who in turn, gives two of her candy bars to the first girl. How many candy bars do they have left between them?

## Chapter 2 - Questions

**29.** With my face paint and squeaky nose, I should bring people a lot of joy. But instead, I scare the daylights out of people, especially with my crazy laugh.

**What am I?**

**30.** Two vampires are standing on a scale, each holding ten pints of blood. Vampire 1 weighs ten pounds more than vampire 2. They want the scales to read the same. Vampire 1 puts down ten pounds of blood while vampire 2 picks up ten pounds of blood.

**Will they weigh the same?**

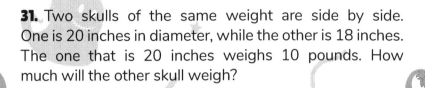

**Chapter 2 - Questions**

**31.** Two skulls of the same weight are side by side. One is 20 inches in diameter, while the other is 18 inches. The one that is 20 inches weighs 10 pounds. How much will the other skull weigh?

**32.** Why can't a cyclops wear an eyepatch?

**33.** Most creatures – dead or alive – are terrified of zombies. Why did the skeleton and the scarecrow feel safe around the zombie?

**34.** I am full but am not a glass. I am white but not milk. I glow but am not a light bulb.

**What am I?**

**35.** A witch is walking around at night carrying a broomstick.

**Why is this unusual?**

**36.** I am a piece of clothing, often worn by those of a mysterious nature, such as a wizard. I can come in designs, or just be dark. I can be used to hide someone or just protect them from the elements.

**What am I?**

**37.** The sewer and a cozy subway track are my sweet abodes. I'll take any creepy dirty home.

**What am I?**

## Halloween Fun Facts

When you go trick or treating on Halloween, do you know approximately how many calories your candy bag contains at the end of the night? On average, 11,000 calories!

**38.** A boy goes out trick or treating and wants to completely disguise himself. He puts on a wig, different clothing and completely covers up his arms and legs. People still recognize him.

**Why is that?**

**Chapter 2 - Questions**

**39.** A vampire works the night shift at the blood bank. One night, he is scheduled to work from 7pm until 7pm the following night.

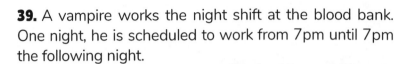

## Why is this a problem?

**40.** There are two ways to become a zombie. One way is to be a reawakened corpse. What is the other way? (Hint: Don't bite on this one too hard.)

## Chapter 2 - Questions

**41.** The Grim Reaper goes to an old apparition and a young man in his early 20s.

### Which one would he take?

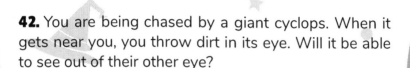

**42.** You are being chased by a giant cyclops. When it gets near you, you throw dirt in its eye. Will it be able to see out of their other eye?

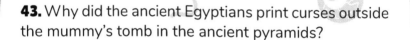

**43.** Why did the ancient Egyptians print curses outside the mummy's tomb in the ancient pyramids?

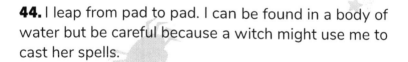

**44.** I leap from pad to pad. I can be found in a body of water but be careful because a witch might use me to cast her spells.

### What am I?

**45.** When you're asleep at night, I am the visions you see that give you a fright.

### What am I called?

**Chapter 2** - Questions

**46.** I am long and made of wood. I am mainly used by witches and wizards to perform magic.

**What am I?**

---

**47.** Once inside, there is no escape. It does not matter, though, because whoever is inside of me is not living anyway. I am large and made of a strong wood. Strong enough to carry a large human.

**What am I?**

**48.** Along your spine, there's more than nine. Branching bones give your lung a home.

**What are they?**

---

**49.** If you are running towards a ghost at 100 miles per hour, how hard will the collision be?

**50.** If you're trying to catch a bat, how will you bait the trap?

**51.** Why did the werewolf let the third-place runner pass him near the finish line?

**52.** A stony sight, a moat of plight, chambers and a lair. Here is where you'll find my liege, trespassers beware.

**Where is this?**

**53.** What would be the first thing a mummy would buy from a pharmacy?

**54.** I am the type of bat who is named after my mythical alter ego.

**What kind of bat am I?**

**55.** I am the portal the Celtics believed the undead were able to use to get back to earth on October 31. Some people can make me with their nose; all of you make me with your clothes.

**What am I?**

# Halloween Fun Facts

Do you think that Pumpkins have always been carved on Halloween? Initially turnips were carved. But then, Irish immigrants used pumpkins because they were less expensive than turnips, and they made delicious pies and soups.

**56.** This was once alive but now feeds on the living. It walks haggard step. With thoughts of brain for dinner, his mouth is wet from frothing.

**What is it?**

**Chapter 2** - Questions

**57.** At what point is a werewolf and witch the same?

**58.** I am driven by Dullahan, the Irish fairy of death. I have a six-horse-power engine. Unlike the one Cinderella had, I will never be a pumpkin.

**What am I?**

## Chapter 2 - Questions

**59.** Over 2000 years ago the Celts, a people in Ireland, France, and the United Kingdom, celebrated New Year's Eve on me. I marked the end of the summer and harvest, and the beginning of winter. Because one year blurred into the next, people thought spirits could escape from the world of the dead to join the world of the living. They created huge bonfires to keep these spirits away. Today I am still a day of celebration, but with pumpkins instead of bonfires.

### What day am I?

**60.** The treats people gave to the poor on Halloween in the 1600's had nothing to do with the feet, but it sure sounded like they did.

### What were they called?

**61.** I am what happens when the hairs on your arms stand up. When you get nervous, your skin shows it. I am what happens when you get terrified and there is no way to hide it.

### What am I called?

**62.** Scary creatures made of stone will guard your entire palace. Their evil eyes, wings and claws reveal their seething malice.

### What are they?

**63.** I am a benevolent being. Often I look like a human but I am depicted with wings.

**What am I?**

**64.** I am a science experiment, but I am not a chemical. I come to life with electricity, but I am not a light bulb. I have bolts but am not lightening.

**What am I?**

**65.** A vampire can only drink a certain amount of blood. What is the most important thing they need in order to get blood?

_____

**66.** The full moon is out as you are walking down the street. Suddenly, all the lights go out.

### How can you still see?

_____

**67.** Emily saw a ghost on October 31st. She had already seen this ghost multiple times on the 31st. This is her first time seeing the ghost today.

### How is this possible?

_____

**68.** Jack tricked Satan by talking the devil into climbing a tree. He then engraved the sign of the cross on the tree so Satan could not get down. When Jack died, Satan would not allow him into Hell, and the trickster Jack certainly wasn't good enough to qualify for Heaven. What happened to Jack and why is the Jack O'lantern named after him?

_____

**69.** If the undead choose not to return to the area in which they lived, they usually visit two particular types of people. Exactly who do the undead choose to visit? (Hint, The answer is somewhat relative.)

**Chapter 2** - Questions

**70.** A vampire is walking around. He has cramps and is feeling weak. He is obviously dehydrated. What would you call this?

**71.** When a skeleton and a ghoul sit down to watch a scary movie, who will leave first?

**72.** Just like their name may suggest, werewolves are very good with directions.

**Why is that?**

## Chapter 2 - Questions

**73.** There was a monster under your bed, but when you looked, it was empty. There was a monster in your closet and when you looked, it was empty. There was a monster in the hallway and when you looked, it was empty. There is a monster everywhere you just looked, how is this possible?

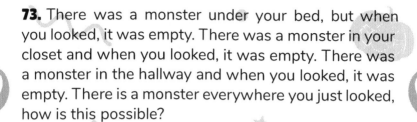

**74.** I am huge and ugly, and I like to eat human flesh, especially that of children and babies. I am known to lie; in fact, I'm a can of bull, if you get the pun. The first part of my name sounds as if we are finished, that things are completed or over. When you say the second part of name, you sound a little like a tiger.

### What am I?

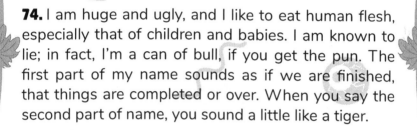

**75.** A black cat makes a bet that she can jump off the roof multiple times and still survive. For each jump, she gets $100. She jumps a total of eight times.

### Why did she stop there?

**76.** Tradition says that the first girl to get an apple from the tub would be the first to get one of these, a special type of band.

### What was it?

**77.** I am a type of bird who stays awake all night. People always wonder "Hoo" I am.

**What am I?**

**78.** In the middle ages, people were advised to stay home on Halloween because that was the night the ghosts came out. If you had to go outside, you would want to wear me. I would ensure that you would look like a ghost, allowing you to blend in with other ghosts until you could get safely back home.

**What am I?**

## Chapter 2 - Questions

**79.** I am home to some, but not a house. I have paths but am not a park. I welcome visitors in the day, but don't come around by dark.

### What am I?

**80.** If you give me to a witch, she will love you, as I would be her main form of transport. However, you also created a way for her to keep terrorizing the town's people.

### What am I?

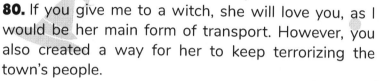

**81.** The first ghost story by an American author was Washington Irving's the Legend of Sleepy Hollow. In that story, what type of ghost is the schoolteacher, Icabod Crane, chased by? (Hint: Hold your horses; don't lose your head trying to solve this.)

**82.** By chasing Icabod Crane, what does the Headless Horseman hope to accomplish? (Hint: You and I sometimes say that we want to do it too.)

**83.** If you run into a warlock, a male witch, you will run into me. Warlocks are accused of "practicing" me, but, to be honest, they don't need any practice. When I am around, things usually end tragically, so it is only fitting that my name rhyme with "tragic".

### What am I?

**Chapter 2 - Questions**

**84.** A witch is stirring cold liquid for a person she has kidnapped. How does the person know she is doing it wrong?

**85.** I am a person who eats another person. At the beginning of history I was very respected because I had a way of making dead loved ones ones a part of you. Today, of course, it is illegal to have your teacher for dinner, and even buttering up the teacher is frowned upon. **What am I?**

## Chapter 2 - Questions

**86.** I appear in folklore as either a dwarf or a giant; never as an ordinary-sized person. I live in caves and under bridges. Today, I am the creature that "flames" people on their computer; someone who provokes others into being very emotional. **What is it?**

# Halloween Fun Facts

Do you know what you can get a $1,000 fine for on Halloween? Using Silly Strings in Hollywood! It has been banned there since 2004, because people bought it and made all the streets a mess.

**87.** If a car full of vampires are in a rollover accident, where would you bury the ones who survived?

## Chapter 2 - Questions

**88.** I am a fancy intricate structure made by an 8-legged creature. I am strong but soft. People often walk into me unexpectedly.

**89.** Fear this haunting hooded guy, the man is a real creeper. He collects you at your "time" He's known as the ____.

## Chapter 2 - Questions

**90.** I like to cause horrible trouble, I'll gladly take the blame. You know me by a few things, like "he-who-shall-not-be-named."

**Who am I?**

**91.** A vampire, a skeleton and a jack-o-lantern walk into a medical center. Who will they most likely see to treat them.

**92.** I am the reason witches wear those tall black hats. You may find the hats scary looking, but that is not the reason the witches wear them. The witches coven is very good at marketing, and real-world witches used the hat as a marketing gimmick to sell their wares in the marketplace. The answer to this riddle is head-and-shoulders above other possible answers.

**What am I?**

**93.** I have a concealed crown with a wide brim, but I am not used for ice-cream. Witches see the point to me.

**What am I?**

**94.** A man with no arms wants to carve a Jack-O-Lantern.

**How will he do it?**

**95.** What is the perfect profession for a ghost who loves to write books?

**96.** I look just like the substance in all of us that sustains life, but I am just really some water and red dye. Put me on and people will believe you are hurt.

**What am I?**

**97.** I am a small black creature, scary to see. You are most likely to see me at night. I live in a cave and sleep upside down.

## What am I?

**98.** A vampire can live forever, But which of their body parts will wear down first?

**99.** What were the financially poor people who received the party treats on Halloween in the 1600's supposed to do in exchange for receiving the treat? If you or I were to see these cake eaters, we would think they had earbuds and cellphones on them.

## Chapter 2 - Questions

**100.** How do vampires cast spells?

**101.** I am the holiday the Celtics celebrated on October 31. You will celebrate me on December 31. Don't drop the ball!

**What am I?**

**Chapter 2 - Questions**

**102.** Maia and Jane were walking through a corn maze. They knew that the werewolf was nearby when they looked down into the dirt.

**How did they know?**

---

# Halloween Fun Facts

If you were a Roman would you be celebrating Halloween in October? No, you'd celebrate Feralia – a 9-day festival to celebrate dead souls and spirits, and this took place in February.

---

**103.** A candy that will rot your teeth, a dentist's favorite treat. Chewy, sticky, hard to handle, so yummy with chocolate or when on top of your apple.

**What candy is this?**

## Chapter 2 - Answers

1. Nothing. You won't miss losing nothing. You will be poor if you have nothing and you will starve if you eat nothing

2. Trombone

3. There is no upstairs from the main floor. While there are two stories, one of them is the basement.

4. They weigh the same

5. Take away the G

6. Cemetery

7. Potion

8. Beast

9. Blood bank

10. Cemetery gates

11. Garlic

12. Halloween decorations

13. Their breath

14. Howl

15. A dungeon

16. Dia de Los Muertos/Day of the dead

17. Cauldron

18. There is too much iron in the blood

19. Wizard

20. Raw eggs

21. The letter N

22. None of them. They are all flying

23. The door is still closed. He needs to open it

24. Headless horseman

25. Skull

26. Coffin

27. Corn maze

28. They still have 10. They were just traded in between the three

29. The zombie wanted brains, and neither the skeleton or the scarecrow have any.

30. No, the two vampires just switched weights.

31. Also 10 pounds

32. They only have one eye

33. The wind blew the magic dust away. It never landed on the man

34. A full moon

35. She should be riding it

36. Cloak

37. A rat

38. He did not cover his face

## Chapter 2 - Answers

39. He would not be able to work from 7 PM to 7 AM because this would involve working during the day and vampires are afraid of daylight.

40. Being bitten by a zombie.

41. The young man. An apparition is non-living.

42. Nope. Once again, a cyclops only has one eye.

43. To discourage grave robbers from taking the possession that is buried with the corpse

44. A toad

45. Nightmare

46. Magic wand

47. Casket

48. Ribs

49. There will be no collision. It is a ghost. You will run right through it.

50. Pint of blood

51. The second place winner received a silver medal, and werewolves hate silver

52. A castle

53. Bandages

54. Vampire bat

55. Wrinkle (in time)

56. A zombie

57. The first letter, "W"

58. Coach

59. October 31

60. Soul cake

61. Goosebumps

62. Gargoyles

63. An angel

64. Frankenstein's monster

65. Their fangs

66. Because of the moonlight

67. She always saw the ghost on the 31st, but not all in one year.

68. He wanders the earth carrying a carved turnip with an undying ember of Hell in it.

69. Friends and relatives.

70. Bloodthirsty

71. A skeleton. They don't have the guts

72. Werewolves always know "where" they are going. They have a great sense of smell

73. Empty is the monster's name

74. Ogre

75. The cat has nine lives and already used up eight

# Chapter 2 - Answers

76. A husband
77. Owl
78. Mask
79. A cemetery
80. A new broomstick
81. Goosebumps
82. He wants to get a head [and we want to get ahead]
83. Magic
84. The cauldron is not bubbling
85. Cannibal
86. Troll
87. You won't bury the ones who survived.
88. Spider-web

89. Grim reaper
90. Lord Voldemort
91. The vampire will see the dentist for his fangs, the skeleton will see the orthopedist for his bones, and the jack-o-lantern will see a psychiatrist because he feels hollow inside.
92. To be seen
93. Little red riding hood
94. It's a Jack-O-Lantern which means it's already carved
95. Ghost writing

96. Witch's hat
97. Bat
98. Their fangs
99. Pray for the giver.
100. Vampires do not cast spells
101. New Year's Eve
102. Saw his footprints
103. Caramel

# Chapter 3

# Riddles to Make You Scream!

"Just because I cannot see it, doesn't mean I can't believe it."

~ Jack Skellington
– Nightmare before Christmas

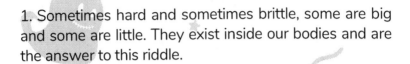

## Chapter 3 - Questions

1. Sometimes hard and sometimes brittle, some are big and some are little. They exist inside our bodies and are the answer to this riddle.

**What are they?**

**2.** I sit on top of the sorcerer's head. I have no magic within me, and yet he is rarely seen in public without me. My presence tells those around them that he is a sorcerer.

**What am I?**

3. I have a face but no ears. I have two or three hands, and my so-called second hand is really my third hand. I am old. My grandchildren frequently have no hands at all. I love to tock. Do you want to learn about my ticks? I am known for my striking, but I promise not to hit you. I make people aware of when it is midnight by playing a loud gong.

**What am I?**

4. Jim, Terry, and Sarah enter a haunted house. They get trapped inside, where there is no electricity. The sun is about to go down, and they need to escape all the ghouls. The only way out is to fight, and they can only have one weapon of their choice. Jim picks up a metal pipe. Terry grabs a chainsaw with a very long extension cord. Sarah grabs a knife.

**Which one of them will not escape?**

## Chapter 3 - Questions

**5.** I am a ghostly figure, but you often see me right after someone passes.

### What am I?

**6.** I am the sound the floorboards make in the haunted house, and perhaps in your house too. My name reminds many people of a small river .

**7.** There were 12 men at a pumpkin patch. There were 12 pumpkins. Each grabs a pumpkin. There are 11 pumpkins remaining. How is this possible?

**8.** There are two fathers and two sons. Together, they buy three pumpkins. Each person leaves with one pumpkin.

### How is this possible?

**9.** A ghost and a werewolf are standing on an empty road late at night. Suddenly, a truck comes out of nowhere. The werewolf shields himself by standing behind the ghost.

### What happened next?

**10.** Casper the Ghost was about to leave his house to meet his friends at the haunted shopping mall. Suddenly it started to rain. Casper decides to stay home. **Why is that?**

**11.** A man who lives in a completely circular house is suspected of stealing pumpkins when his neighbor finds a bunch in his house that look like his own. When he confronted the man, the man said he had them in the corner of his house before but just brought them out. How did the neighbor know the man was lying?

**12.** A ghost is a spirit and usually requires a sheet to be seen. I am a full-bodied spirit that can be seen without resorting to a sheet. People can literally see right through me. The first part of my name sounds like an admirer of a sports player. The second part of my name sound like a two-thousand pound weight.

**What am I?**

**13.** A family of witches is living in a house. The daughter witch wants to go out at night. The mom witch forbids her and tells her to stay in her room. The daughter goes upstairs, grabs her broom from the closet, and then puts some pillows under her bedsheets to make it seem like she was sleeping under them. She then flies out. Later in the night, the mom comes in and sees her daughter sleeping under her sheets, so she closes her bedroom door quietly to avoid waking her up. The mom witch then goes to get something from the closet. This is when she realized her daughter is not home. How did she know?

**14.** The person who buys this will not need it, while the person who lays in it, will not know what it feels like.

**What is it?**

**15.** A word that means creepy but also the name of a Great Lake.

**What is the word?**

**Chapter 3** - Questions

**16.** How do you retrace the steps of a pumpkin that has gone missing?

**17.** Your light in the house goes out during a thunderstorm. It is pitch black. You need to find some candles. What is a better option to help you search, a flashlight with low battery power or a lantern that has a very bright light when it's on?

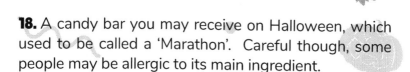

**18.** A candy bar you may receive on Halloween, which used to be called a 'Marathon'. Careful though, some people may be allergic to its main ingredient.

### What is this?

**19.** A teacher is suspected of committing a crime on Halloween night. When questioned about where he was, he said he was his teaching class. Is this teacher telling the truth?

**20.** I will act like I am serious when I am doing this, but I am really being conniving and will trick you at your own expense. What is it I'm doing?

**21.** I am often child's favorite treat because I last the longest after eating. You can chew me, but you shouldn't swallow me.

### What am I?

**22.** A woman was walking, when somebody pinched her arm. She looked back and saw nobody. Then she tripped and fell and looked up and saw nobody. Then she was pushed into a wall and turned around and saw nobody. Finally, she yelled at them to stop.

### Who was she yelling at?

**Chapter 3** - Questions

**22.** I will pull out your teeth against your will. Come to me after eating all that candy and you will wish you had received toothpaste instead.

**Who am I?**

**24.** Why would vampires and ghouls make the perfect organ donors?

**Chapter 3 - Questions**

**25.** While trick-or-treating, a little boy in his vampire costume goes to his very first house, and the owner gives him two candy bars. A little boy goes to the same house for his first stop in a ghost costume. The owner gives him two candy bars. A little boy goes to his first house in a monster costume and gets two candy bars. When this little boy looks in his bag, he has a total of six candy bars. How is this possible if it was the first house for the boy in a monster costume?

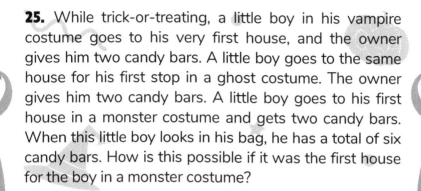

**26.** A woman meets a witch, and the witch offers her a drink. The woman is very concerned. The drink looks normal. It is water with ice cubes. But she is still concerned. The drink may be poisoned. The witch tells her not to worry. She even takes a drink herself. In fact, she drinks all of it quickly, leaving behind the ice cubes. At this point, the woman takes a glass. She sips on it slowly though as she is still concerned. Shortly after finishing it, the woman collapses. Why is the witch alright if she had the same drink?

**27.** If you have five pumpkins and you carve three, how many do you have left?

**28.** Do you know why vampires' favorite past time is baseball?

**29.** A boy has a regular sized Snickers bar and a regular sized Twix. He wants to eat two pieces of candy now and save one for later.

**How will he do it?**

**30.** I am the animal that carries Death, a skeleton, in the Apocalypse. There are four of my kind in John's Revelation, each carrying a different rider. If you yell too loudly at the haunted house this weekend, people may say you are a little one of me. **What am I?**

# Halloween Fun Facts

Do you know why people wear Halloween costumes? It comes from Celtic and European traditions, whereby they wanted to hide from spirits who returned on October 31st, so they wore masks and costumes, to trick the spirits into believing they were ghosts too.

**31.** You will find me at the cemetery every day. As my name suggests, I take care, and I am known for my hard work. My duties at the cemetery include pulling weeds and mowing. I am a manager, and last I checked, I had 600 people under me.

**Who am I?**

## Chapter 3 - Questions

**32.** On a frightful Halloween night, you get jumped and ambushed by a werewolf. You get bitten. The next month, on a full moon, you worry about getting bitten by the same werewolf. What is wrong with this scenario?

_____

**33.** How will you be able to distinguish a vampire's shadow when walking outside?

_____

**34.** In October, how can you assure that you will stay awake all day, every day?

_____

**35.** Which three creatures would you combine to make to the perfect body?

_____

**36.** A vampire goes into a grocery store and begins checking out the vegetables. Suddenly, he feels dizzy.

**What happened?**

**37.** A headless horseman rides into town with his horse Friday, terrorizes the townsmen, and then leaves on Friday. How did he do it?

**38.** A vampire will always refuse to come to your house for breakfast but would love a good late-night dinner.

**Why is that?**

## Chapter 3 - Questions

**39.** After Halloween, a boy goes to school with ten pieces of candy. His mother tells him not to trade the candies with anyone. The boy figured if he comes back with the same number of candies, his mom will not know. So, he traded the candies with his friends, and he came home with 10 pieces of candy. His mom knows that he traded the candies.

### How does she know?

**40.** Two vampires sit down for a meal. One eats expired ham, and the other one eats fresh garlic parmesan bread.

### Who will get sick?

**41.** Turn left, then right, then round-about. Two lefts, then a stop. You've found the zombie's house.

### Where is it?

**42.** A vampire and a werewolf walk by a giant magnet. The werewolf walks right by and keeps going. The vampire slows down significantly.

### Why?

**Chapter 3** - Questions

**43.** Two living corpses are walking around town. One is identified, the other is a mystery.

**What are they?**

**44.** You are chasing a few ghosts as they are running through a forest full of trees. As they move around the trees, you realize that they are not real ghosts. How so?

## Chapter 3 - Questions

**45.** If a pumpkin leaves the scene of a crime, what evidence suggests it was involved?

**46.** In the cemetery, it is considered bad manners to do this on a grave. Not only is it disrespectful, but it also may disturb the sleep of those who are underground. People have prayed that these sleepers "rest in peace", and if you do this on the grave those who have gone before are not resting in peace. My name is not "talk", but it does rhyme with "talk".

**What am I?**

**47.** I am the direction most graves will face in a Christian cemetery. The ancient Egyptians also buried their mummies facing this direction. In both cases it was because the Son was going to come from this direction on the final day. So, which am I - north, south, east, or west?

**48.** I am the substance that comprises the witch's caldron, that big black pot they use to make their potions. None of their ingredients bother me. To be honest, you actually want a little of me in your diet each day; I am good for your blood stream. My nickname is "Fe", or at least I'm told that periodically. A superhero is named after me.

**Who am I?**

**Chapter 3** - Questions

**49.** James has a three-story house. He wants to place two pumpkins on the first story, four pumpkins on the second story and six pumpkins on the third story. How many will he place on the fourth story?

---

# Halloween Fun Facts

Do you know why orange and black are used for many Halloween decorations? Orange is meant to symbolize autumn leaves, and black is associated with death.

---

**50.** A tall ghost is sitting in a movie theatre right in front of a couple and their view of the screen. Why does this not bother them?

**Chapter 3** - Questions

**51.** Why would a Witch and a Vampire make a perfect couple?

**52.** I am a stone slab found in front of a tomb in many cemeteries. My name makes me sound as if I am a leader, but none of my peers believe I am more important than they are. I am a stone that marks a grave. Don't get me confused with the tombstone, the rock that literally covers the stone tomb.

**What am I?**

**53.** I have multiple legs like a spider. I mostly live in the desert. One sting from my curvy tail and you could be paralyzed.

**What am I?**

**54.** A guy is standing in front of a mirror fixing his hair. Suddenly, he feels a tap from behind from his vampire friend. How come he did not see him coming?

**Chapter 3** - Questions

**55.** A skeleton with no arms goes to a party with his friend. His friend is so tired by the end of the night that he can't even walk. The skeleton picks him up and carries him in front of him. How did he do it?

**56.** What will you not have yet on the morning of Halloween?

## Chapter 3 - Questions

**57.** Three friends walk into a dark cave. After they are inside, the entryway collapses. Which one of the three friends survive?

---

**58.** Mike is walking with someone else on a dirt path at night. You're walking behind them. You look down, notice something missing, and immediately know that something is not right.

### What do you notice?

---

**59.** Most people throw me away at the Halloween season, which is a gutsy move, considering I am not really trash. I can be used as a batter for fish or lamb; I can be turned into pesto or used with guacamole to flavor your favorite Mexican dish. I can be used to flavor bread; and I can be eaten alone. I can also be planted, so that a new crop will grow next year. You may call your sweetheart by my first name, but don't ever call her the second part of my name because it is a little bit seedy.

### What am I?

---

**60.** A witch has been roaming the town. What is the least useful way to track the witch?

## Chapter 3 - Questions

**61.** An elderly man recently had all his teeth taken out. He needs to wear dentures. One evening, he is bobbing for apples at a Halloween party with his grandkids. He bites into an apple, but nothing comes up as he removes his mouth. Beside the apple, something else of his is also missing.

### What is missing?

**62.** You meet a werewolf outside. He falls and scrapes his knee. You see him several days later with the scrape on his knee. At this point, you know he is not a real werewolf.

### How do you know this?

## Chapter 3 - Questions

**63.** I am Cerberus, the legendary creature who guards the entrance to the underworld. I have three heads; try to get away. Those who have seen me and were fortunate enough to escape say that I have red demon-like eyes. They also say that I smell of brimstone, which is probably how I got the first part of my name. I am not man's best friend, nor am I man's "beast" friend; in fact, I am not your friend at all. Don't even think about taking me hunting or birding; don't bring your kids to rub my belly. I refuse to be domesticated!

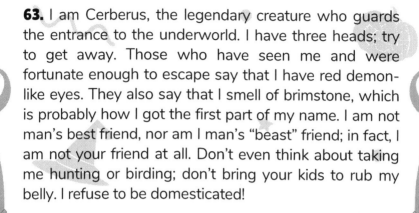

**What am I?**

_____

**64.** If you get bitten by a werewolf and nothing happens to you. What does this mean?

_____

**65.** I should be orange, like so many of us are on Halloween, but if you see me looking yellow, then you know something is wrong.

**What am I?**

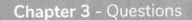

**Chapter 3** - Questions

**66.** How was Suzie able to get the skeleton to laugh?

**67.** A black raven with a white stripe on its left wing flies over a man's house and makes a large screeching noise. The next day, there is a raven on the man's porch, but he knew it was not the same raven.

**How could he tell?**

## Chapter 3 - Questions

**68.** What is a werewolf's least favorite piece of jewelry?

# Halloween Fun Facts

Did you know that there used to be a romantic element to Halloween? Women used to play games on Halloween with the intention of finding out about their future husband. Bits of apple skins were thrown over their shoulders and the shape the scrap landed in, would predict their husband's initials. There was apple bobbing, and the first to succeed would be the first to marry. Hazelnuts were also burned to determine the success of a relationship. If they burned long and well, that was better than if they sputtered and fizzled out.

**69.** Where can you find a ghost, a vampire, a doctor, a nurse, a dentist, a baseball player, and a werewolf all in one spot?

**Chapter 3 - Questions**

**70.** How do you trap a ghost?

**71.** You see me at lunch, and I am wearing a cape, my face is white, I have large fangs, and I have no garlic. How do you know I am not a real vampire?

## Chapter 3 - Questions

**72.** A boy lives on the bottom of a hill. He comes out of his front door and wants to roll his pumpkin down the hill. When he puts it on the ground, it does not move.

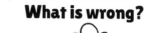

**What is wrong?**

**73.** There is a search for a missing vampire who has been stalking you. You walked into a butcher shop and found a piece of evidence linking to the culprit.

**What did you find**

## Chapter 3 - Questions

**74.** How did the ghost repair the rip in the sheet?

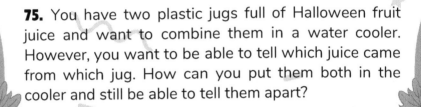

**75.** You have two plastic jugs full of Halloween fruit juice and want to combine them in a water cooler. However, you want to be able to tell which juice came from which jug. How can you put them both in the cooler and still be able to tell them apart?

**76.** A witch is deciding on whether to buy a new hat rack or new auto insurance. Which is the better option?

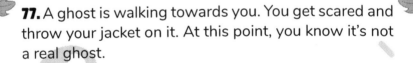

**77.** A ghost is walking towards you. You get scared and throw your jacket on it. At this point, you know it's not a real ghost.

## Why is that?

**78.** Frankenstein's monster is walking next to you, and you turn and look him in the eye. How do you know that he is not a real monster?

## Chapter 3 - Questions

**79.** It is a full moon. As the moon comes out, your friend tells you a story about how he once got bitten by a werewolf. It is a very descriptive story that takes over an hour to tell. It is very believable the way he makes it out. How do you know that it's not true?

**80.** As parents are folding bedsheets, they realize that their kids were making their own Halloween costumes to go as ghosts. How did they figure this out?

**Chapter 3 - Questions**

**81.** A child witch goes to school on her broom. The rain is coming down hard. She decides to go out with friends after school and when she comes home, she lies to her mom and tells her she was caught in a flood. How did the mom know she was lying?

**82.** A witch, a vampire, and a ghost need to clean their house. What job would you give to the witch?

**83.** A witch with a bald head is convicted of committing a crime. Which piece of clothing was found on the scene?

**84.** I am a battlefield formation comprised of two or more divisions. Put an "e" at the end of my name, though, and I am a dead body. Many of the soldiers in the opposing armies will likely be me when the battle is over. What is my name?

# Halloween Fun Facts

Why do you get candy on Halloween? It originates from around 1200 A.D in Britain, Ireland and Europe on the 31st of October, soul cakes were made (using saffron and currants) to both show respect for and to distract spirits. Beggars would go from home to home asking the people there for soul cakes, and in return would pray for their relatives who had passed away.

**85.** A man is walking with a sharp silver box in front of him. Out of the bushes, pops a werewolf. The werewolf attacks the man and the man gets on the ground. At this point, the werewolf stops and back away. Why?

**Chapter 3 - Questions**

**86.** Two pumpkins are growing on a tree. One is five pounds, and one is ten pounds. If they both fall at the same time, which one will hit first?

**87.** You meet a vampire walking out of a restaurant. He is eating garlic bread, has giant fangs, and drinking a glass of blood. He walks towards you, but you do not worry.

**Why is this?**

## Chapter 3 - Answers

1. Bones
2. The sorcerer's hat
3. Grandfather's clock
4. Terry. His chainsaw will not turn on, as there is no power.
5. Wraith
6. Creak
7. Each is the man's name. So, Each grabs one of the pumpkins, and there are 11 more remaining.
8. A grandfather, who is also a father, and his son, who is also a father to his son, buy the pumpkins. So, between the three, you have two fathers and two sons.
9. The werewolf still got hit. The truck went right through the ghost, which is just a spirit and not solid.
10. This is because Casper is a ghost. Ghosts hate the rain. It dampens their spirits.
11. He lives in a completely circular house. There are no corners.
12. Phantom
13. Her daughter's broom is not in the closet.
14. Apparition
15. Eerie/Erie
16. Pumpkins don't take steps. It is something else. Run for it!
17. The flashlight. Since you don't have candles, you can't use the lantern.
18. Snickers candy bar
19. No, there is no class on Halloween night.
20. Prank
21. Gum
22. Nobody. That is the name of the person who kept causing the accidents.
23. An evil dentist.

## Chapter 3 - Answers

24. Vampires have all types of blood, and ghouls have all types of flesh.

25. It was the same boy all three times; he just changed his costume.

26. The drink was poisoned. The poison was in the ice cubes. The witch drank it quickly before the ice cubes had a chance to melt.

27. Five. The pumpkins are still there, just carved.

28. This is because every night they turn into bats.

29. Eat the Twix and save the Snickers. Remember, Twix comes in two to a package.

30. Horse.

31. Cemetery Caretaker

32. You are a werewolf yourself now, so you don't have to worry about getting bitten again by the same werewolf. This time, you do the biting.

33. You won't. Vampires only go out at night.

34. Sleep during the night

35. The skeleton because it has the bones, the vampires because they have the blood and ghouls because they have the flesh.

36. Walked by the garlic.

37. His horse's name is Friday

38. Vampires don't go out in the daytime.

39. He still has the same number of pieces, but different candies. Of course, why wouldn't he just eat them?

40. The one who ate the garlic parmesan. It does not matter about the expired food.

41. The dead end

42. Because of the iron in his body from all the blood

43. One is a zombie, while the other is a mummy.

44. They are moving around the trees rather than going through them.

45. A green stem

46.   Walk (never walk on a grave)
47.   East
48.   Iron (and that superhero, of course, is Iron Man)
49.   There is no fourth story
50.   They can see right through the ghost
51.   One provides the meal, the other provides transportation.
52.   Headstone.
53.   Scorpion
55.   Because the vampire had no reflection
55.   He didn't. He has no arms.
56.   Your candy from trick or treating.
57.   They all do. Only the entry way collapsed, and they were all already inside.
58.   There is only one set of footprints.
59.   Pumpkin seeds
60.   Looking for her footprints because witches just fly.
61.   His dentures
62.   The scrape is still on his knee. Werewolves heal very fast.
63.   Hell Hound
64.   You were not really bitten by a werewolf.
65.   An unhealthy pumpkin.
66.   She touched its funny bone.
67.   There is no white stripe on the wing.
68.   A silver necklace
69.   A Halloween party.
70.   You can't. They will move through anything.
71.   I am out during lunch time.
72.   The boy lives on the bottom of the hill. It has nowhere to go.
73.   Beef jerky. There are marks on the meat and all the blood sucked out

## Chapter 3 - Answers

74. With a pumpkin patch

75. Freeze one of the jugs. Pour the liquid water from one jug into the cooler. Cut away the plastic jug of the other and dump the ice in. You will be able to tell them apart.

76. The hat rack is essential. Auto insurance is not essential because they fly on their broomsticks.

77. The jacket stays on them.

78. You can see his eyes, and he is the same height as you.

79. Your friend does not turn into a werewolf while telling the story.

80. There are eye holes in the sheets

81. She has a broom and could have just flown home.

82. Sweeping the floors. They are already familiar with brooms.

83. A pointy hat.

84. Corps

85. He was struck by the box made of silver, the werewolves' one weakness.

86. Can't answer. Pumpkins don't grow on trees.

87. He's eating garlic. You know he's not a real vampire.

# Did you enjoy the book?

If you did, we are ecstatic. If not, please write your complaint to us and we will ensure we fix it.

If you're feeling generous, there is something important that you can help me with – tell other people that you enjoyed the book.

Ask a grown-up to write about it on Amazon. When they do, more people will find out about the book. It also lets Amazon know that we are making kids around the world laugh. Even a few words and ratings would go a long way.

If you have any ideas or jokes that you think are super funny, please share them with us. We would love to hear from you. Our email address is -

riddleland@riddlelandforkids.com

**bonus book**

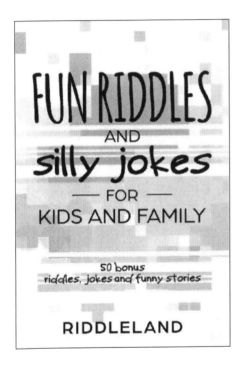

# FUN RIDDLES
### AND
## silly jokes
#### — FOR —
#### KIDS AND FAMILY

50 bonus
riddles, jokes and funny stories

**RIDDLELAND**

SCAN ME

## https://pixelfy.me/riddlelandbonus

Thank you for buying this book. As a token of our
appreciation, we would like to offer a special bonus - a
collection of 50 original jokes, riddles and funny stories

# CONTEST

## Would you like your jokes and riddles to be featured in our next book?

We are having a contest to discover the most clever and funny boys and girls in the world!

**1) Creative and Challenging Riddles**
**2)Tickle Your Funny Bone Contest**

Parents, please email us your child's "Original" Riddle or Joke, **and he or she could win a $25 Amazon gift card and be featured in our next book.**

### Here are the rules:

1) We're looking for super challenging riddles and extra funny jokes

2) Jokes and riddles MUST be 100% original - NOT something discovered on the internet.

3) You can submit both a joke and a riddle as they are two separate contests.

4) Don't get help from your parents - UNLESS they're as funny as you are.

5) Winners will be announced via email or our Facebook group – Riddleland for kids

6) In your entry, please confirm which book you purchased.

7) Email us at Riddleland@riddlelandforkids.com..

# Other Fun Books By Riddleland
## Riddles Series

# Try Not to Laugh Challenge
## Joke Series

# Would You Rather Series

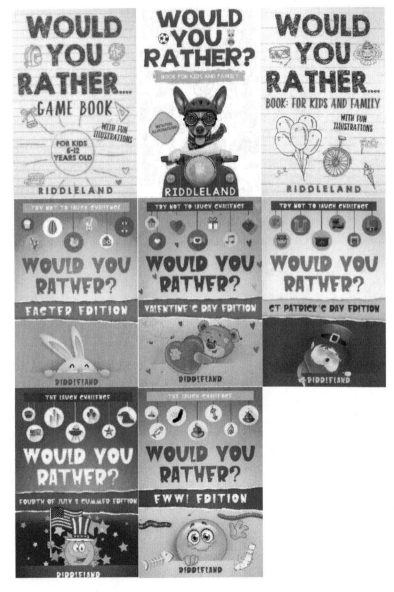

Get them on Amazon or our website at
**www.riddlelandforkids.com**

# Praise for The Dogs

★ "Stratton masterfully constructs a creepy gothic setting... A monstrous, stalking father, unhinging nightmares, a ghostly boy, wild dogs, and a moldy basement add creepy deliciousness to a murder mystery and tale of a boy who, in trying to solve a mystery, may just discover what a loving family might be. An engrossing blend of murder mystery and family story."

—*Kirkus*, Starred Review

"This is an accomplished, gripping, and thoughtful story, whose dramatic ending delivers on every level."

—*The Guardian*

"A real page-turner... [*The Dogs*] stayed with me for days, author Allan Stratton having created an unsettled aura the likes of which Alfred Hitchcock and Stephen King routinely built into their work too... Stratton's depiction of setting and characters is masterful, and his ability to create tension and keep readers on edge is equally strong."

—*Montreal Gazette*

"This is a darkly suspenseful thriller blurring the lines between reality and imagination, keeping you guessing and keeping you awake long into the night listening out for the sound of barking."

—*The Scotsman*, UK

"Stratton's tale of Cameron's attempt to perceive what is real is frightening, but it is his very determination to perceive that fills this novel with a tremendous hope that lingers after the last astonishing scenes."

—Gary D. Schmidt, Michael L. Printz Honor
author and National Book Award finalist

"From the first page, Allan Stratton creates an atmosphere of terror and danger that does not let up till the end… This book deserves to be a hit with not just teen readers but also with anyone who enjoys a good ghostly thriller."

—*We Love This Book Magazine*
(division of *The Bookseller*), UK

"What would it be like if the most frightening thing in your world lay at the heart of your own family? Stratton imagines this horror fully and convincingly."

—*Quill and Quire*, starred review

"It's about ghosts and terrifying danger and going mad all at once. I didn't know what was real and what was imagined until the very last page. I loved it."

—Melvin Burgess, Carnegie Medal winner, *Junk*

"Brilliant, page turning, and eerie. Had me guessing to the very end."

—Joseph Delaney, The Last Apprentice series

# THE DOGS

## ALLAN STRATTON

sourcebooks
fire

Published by Sourcebooks Fire, an imprint of Sourcebooks, Inc.

P.O. Box 4410, Naperville, Illinois 60567-4410

(630) 961-3900

Fax: (630) 961-2168

www.sourcebooks.com

Originally published in 2015 in the United Kingdom by Anderson Press Limited.

Library of Congress Cataloging-in-Publication Data

Stratton, Allan, author.

  The dogs / Allan Stratton. -- [First American edition].

     pages cm

  "Originally published in 2015 in the United Kingdom by Anderson Press Limited."

  Summary: Cameron is used to moving at a moment's notice because he and his mother are always running away from his supposedly violent father, but he is disturbed by their latest refuge, a creepy, deserted farmhouse, haunted by bloodthirsty dogs--and when he sees a boy hiding in the barn, and finds an old picture of the same boy, he starts wondering about the possibility of human ghosts.

  (alk. paper)

  1. Abusive men--Juvenile fiction. 2. Fathers and sons--Juvenile fiction. 3. Mothers and sons--Juvenile fiction. 4. Haunted places--Juvenile fiction. 5. Detective and mystery stories. [1. Mystery and detective stories. 2. Fathers and sons--Fiction. 3. Mothers and sons--Fiction. 4. Haunted places--Fiction.] I. Title.

  PZ7.S9109Do 2015

  823.914--dc23

  [Fic]

2014044059

Printed and bound in the United States of America.

VP 10 9 8 7 6 5 4 3 2 1

For my stepfather, Alex, the best dad in the world

# 1

It's ten p.m. Mom's at the living room window staring at the car across the street. She's been there for an hour. Our lights are out so no one can see her.

I'm downstairs in the rec room playing Zombie Attack. No sound. I don't want Mom to know, although I'm pretty sure she guesses. The longer we're quiet in the dark, the creepier it gets.

*Mom's imagining things.*

But what if she isn't? I focus on the zombies. More silence.

"It's probably nothing," I call up.

"Shh. Keep it down."

"I'm in the basement, Mom. You think someone outside can hear me?"

"Stop it, Cameron. Turn off that game and go to bed."

"Aw, Mom—"

"Cameron."

A zombie jumps from behind a tree and rips my head off. *Thanks, Mom. Way to help me concentrate.* I turn off the game and head up to the living room.

Mom's squeezing her phone. "I'm calling the police."

"Why?" I try to sound normal. "They won't come for hours. By the time they do, whoever's there will be gone."

"It's not 'whoever.' It's him. I know it." She dials.

"Mom, it's a street. People park there."

"Not in neighborhoods where they don't belong. Not opposite the same house three nights in a row. And they don't stay in their car either. It's only a matter of time before he does something. Hello, police?"

I can't breathe. I go upstairs and brush my teeth while Mom gives her name and address to someone who's apparently deaf. The more they tell her to calm down, the angrier she gets.

*Go to bed. Everything's fine.*

Mom's room is at the front of the house. I sneak to her window and peek down at the car. It's out of the light, in the shadow of the trees on the other side of the street. Is there really someone inside?

*Even if there is, so what? They could be waiting for a friend.*

All night?

*It's not against the law to sit in a car.*

That's not the point.

*Stop it. Don't be like her.*

The car drives off like it did last night and the night before that. I go to my room and crawl under the covers. Two hours later the cops arrive.

Mom's ballistic. "I called hours ago. We could be dead."

"Sorry, ma'am. It's been a busy night. Did you get the license number?"

"No, I didn't get the license number. He parks in the shadows. You want me to go out and check with him sitting there waiting for me?"

2

The cops ask more stupid questions. I stick my fingers in my ears and pray for everything to be over.

The cops leave. Mom slams the door. Next thing I know, she's sitting on the side of my bed, holding my hand. "Cameron, honey. We have to go. Get your things."

"Go? What? Now?"

"I don't know how long we've got." She gets up and heads to her room. "He could be anywhere…around the block, who knows. But he'll be back. You can count on it. And the police will be too late."

"Mom—"

"There are things you don't understand, Cameron."

*Oh yeah? I understand lots, Mom. I understand I'm scared, for starters. But why? Because he's tracked us down? Or because you're crazy?*

My clothes are already in a suitcase under my bed; Mom made me pack two days ago, just in case. There's room in the car for our bags, some coats, a box of dishes, some sheets and towels, and the little TV. My grandparents will store the rest of our stuff in their basement. There isn't much, since the places we rent come furnished. I wish we could go to Grandma and Grandpa's. Mom says we can't. She says that's the first place he'd look.

He—him—the guy in the car: Dad.

Mom backs the car onto the street. I look at the house. After a year, I was getting used to the place. This city too. I'd actually started making friends at school. So much for that.

We drive away slowly with the headlights off.

# 2

Mom left Dad when I was eight. She says he'd been acting strange since forever. I have flashes of things, but I'm not sure what's real and what are dreams. And what are things I overheard Mom say to my grandparents.

Anyway, Mom moved us far away. Dad came to see me a few times on supervised visits at some government building. Then all of a sudden we moved again. According to Mom, Dad did things she'll tell me about when I'm older. *So—hey, Mom—when's older? This is our fifth move, and nothing's changed except I'm more messed up than ever.*

Mom says change is great: "Embrace change." It's like her motto or something. Only for Mom, change means planning where to run next before we've even unpacked. From the get-go, she's scouting escape routes "in case of an emergency." So I'm hardly surprised she knows where we're going.

She shows me the virtual tour on her laptop when we stop for gas and a doughnut. "It's perfect. Eight hundred miles away—far enough for us to disappear—the rent's a bargain, and it comes furnished. What do you think?"

"Guess."

"Please don't be like that."

"Mom, it's a farmhouse."

She pretends not to hear me. "The real estate agent says the owner lives on the next farm over if there's ever a problem. He works the land but keeps clear of the house. So we have privacy and security. Isn't that great? Think of the fresh air, the scenery. Think of the fun of exploring the woods beyond those fields."

"How am I going to make any friends on a farm?"

"There's a town not far off that's right by a lake and has a recreation center and a new school and—"

"Hello, I don't drive. I'll have to take the bus home right after."

"Lots of kids take school buses."

I turn away.

Her shoulders sag. "Cameron. You have to try."

"Fine, I'll try. Does 'Farmer Brown' have cows? I'll make friends with them."

Mom closes her laptop. "I know this is hard. But living in the country there's less chance of meeting people who know people who know people. Also it's harder for him to prowl around unnoticed."

"Yeah, right, whatever."

"Cameron, don't give me that look. Please. You know what he did on Facebook. We can't be too careful." She presses her napkin to her eyes.

"Mom, please don't."

"I'm sorry. I can't help it."

Mom freshens up in the bathroom, grabs a coffee for the road, and we drive into the next day. I try to stretch out in the backseat, but it's not as easy as when I was a kid, so I end up playing video games. Mom says it's bad for my eyes, what with all the bouncing around, but I have my earbuds in and pretend not to hear her.

Somehow I fall asleep. I wake up as the sun's going down. Everywhere are cornfields and shadows. "Can we stop someplace? I have to pee."

"Don't worry. We're almost there."

*What? We're moving near here?*

After ten more minutes of country, we pass a high school and football field in the middle of nowhere. A few hundred yards beyond, Mom pulls into an old motel. It's covered in big white shingles, with a little diner at the side and a red vacancy light in the office window.

Up ahead there's an old iron bridge that crosses a river ravine into town and a sign at the side of the road: Welcome to Wolf Hollow.

The room we get is a cheapie, all beige and banged-up furniture, with twin beds, a phone, a TV, and a coffeemaker.

Mom calls Grandma and Grandpa on her phone to let them know we're all right. We never use motel phones—any that aren't ours, for that matter. That's another rule: "If your father bugged Grandma and Grandpa's phone, he could track us down from the motel's number." Mom's made sure both our phones are unlisted so they don't show up on caller ID. She says keeping mine with me at all times is a matter of life and death: "You need to be able to call for help if your father ever attacks you out of nowhere."

"So everything's fine," Mom tells Grandma and Grandpa on

speakerphone. "We're in a really nice motel, and I already have a lead on a terrific house. The agent will be taking us out tomorrow."

"Oh, good," Grandma says. "And how's Cameron?"

I look up from my video game. "Cameron's fine. He's never been better."

Mom gives me a look. She says we always have to sound cheerful when we talk to Grandma and Grandpa. Otherwise they'll worry. Well, if I was Grandma and Grandpa, I'd be worried about things like why we're so happy if we're running from a maniac.

"Seriously, Grandma, this is the best place yet," I say in my *I'm so happy I can hardly believe I'm alive* voice. "One day you'll have to visit. I can't wait."

"Maybe this Christmas?" Grandpa asks. *Right. Like that's going to happen.*

"Let's see what the fall brings," Mom says.

Even when we talk on Skype, these check-ins make me lonely because what we say to each other is totally fake. It's nothing but lies so we can pretend we're feeling things we aren't. I mean, I get we don't want Grandma and Grandpa to worry, and I get they don't want us to *think* they're worrying. But not being honest makes all of us worry even more. With everything a secret, who knows what's real? Not us.

The grandparents I remember were actual people. The ones I talk to now are cardboard cutouts. The more I talk to the cutouts, the less I remember the real ones.

"We'll call again next Sunday," Mom says.

Over and out.

# 3

Mom's in the passenger seat next to the real estate agent, Mr. "Hi-I'm-Ken" Armstrong, a.k.a. C.B.—short for Cowboy Boots. He picked us up after breakfast to show us our new home. Mom says nothing's official until we see it, but I'm not stupid. What I *am* is slouched in the back, wondering how far from town he's going to drive us.

C.B. is super loud and cheery for first thing in the morning. Not to mention for inside a car. He's like the guy with the big warehouse sale on TV, only instead of a ten-second spot he goes on forever and there's no fast-forward.

"The town's called Wolf Hollow," he says, "but there haven't been any wolves since the pioneers cleared the land. There're coyotes, but they keep to themselves pretty much. All the same, you should keep any pets indoors to be safe."

"It's okay. We don't have any," Mom says.

"One thing you *will* have is snow." C.B. grins. "Usually not till November, but we get the odd whiteout in late October. Great for cross-country skiing. Art Sinclair, the landlord, has left an old Ski-Doo in the barn. He says you can use it."

Mom gives me a hopeful smile. "You'd enjoy a Ski-Doo ride, wouldn't you?"

The way she says it, it's like I'm five and she's talking up a ride on the merry-go-round. I stare out the window. "Sure."

"Oh, and Cameron," C.B. announces, "you'll also be pleased to know the town has a new school and a recreation center. There's also a lake—pretty cold, but in summer great for swimming."

I sigh enough for Mom to hear but not enough for her to say anything. "Yeah, I heard." As if C.B. cares what I think. The only reason he included me is so he'd look cool to Mom. *Yeah, way cool, with his boots, leather jacket, and bleached teeth.*

"Here we are," C.B. says like it's Christmas.

We turn onto a gravel lane. The corn's pretty high on either side, so I don't see much till we drive into the yard and get out of the car. Then—

*Whoa! Somebody! Put this place out of its misery!* It's two-story, like in the picture, only you can see things in real life that don't show up on the website. For starters, the bricks are fake, printed on tar paper that ripples under the roof's gutters. Plus the paint on the door and window frames is stripping off. And the yard's a patchwork of potholes, stones, dirt, and crabgrass, stretching back to a wobbly rail fence. The barn beyond is missing a few boards, and the top part slopes to the left.

I toss Mom a *Right, like we're really going to live here* look. She glares a *Behave yourself, Cameron* right back.

"It could use some work," Mom says politely. "But it's not like we're buying."

"Art will do repairs," C.B. says quickly. "His farm is next door. When he was a kid, his father took over the property to double the

Sinclair spread. I think Art lived here for a while, but he moved back to the family home maybe ten years ago, after his parents died. As you can see, he hasn't paid much attention to it since. Even the barn is abandoned." C.B. grins. "Which accounts for the low rent." If he ran a restaurant, he'd serve grilled turd and call it steak.

We cross a sun porch and enter an oversized kitchen. Flowered wallpaper and speckled linoleum are everywhere, and in the center of the room there is a metal table surrounded by six chairs with plaid vinyl seat covers.

On our left are a narrow stairwell going upstairs and a door to the basement. On our right, an archway to the living room and a door to the bathroom. Opposite, a window over the sink looking out to the barn, and a door to the back shed.

Something's missing. A dishwasher. *Seriously. Where's the dishwasher?*

"It's very spacious," Mom says. "I like a big kitchen."

"People spent most of their winters in this room," C.B. tells me, as if I care. "If you look closely, you can see where Mr. Sinclair's plastered over the hole in the ceiling that used to let the heat up to the bedrooms." He looks at Mom. "Come, let me show you the rest."

The rooms on the first floor are laid out in a circle. We cut across the kitchen to the bathroom on the far right. C.B. makes a big deal about the iron tub with claw feet and the washer-dryer that means Mom won't have to do laundry in the basement. He leads us through a door on the opposite wall into the master bedroom.

"What do you think?" He raises the window blind.

"Great view," Mom says. "All those fields and that woods in the distance."

C.B. nods. "Great light too."

Across the bedroom, on the right, is a door to a second narrow staircase and, beyond that, the living room. Mom likes the second stairs. "It's good to have more than one escape route…in case of fire," she adds, but I know what she's *really* thinking.

The living room has a humongous piano and a bunch of old furniture. There's a funky smell from the sofa cushions. At the end is the archway back into the kitchen; we've gone full circle.

Mom and C.B. finish the tour upstairs while I hang behind in the kitchen. I think Mom's glad I've checked out. When I'm in a bad mood, it shows—or, as Mom likes to put it, "You embarrass me and you embarrass yourself."

I stare out the window over the sink. What else can I do?

*Why not check out the basement?*

I open the door and flick on the light switch. The stairs are creaky, the ceiling's low, and the wall plaster's crumbling. It's like going down a passageway into a tomb. I picture a psycho burying a body.

Mom says I freak myself out because I have an imagination. Guess who I got it from? Anyway, if a psycho killer's down here, I can call Mom and C.B.

The basement's cold and damp and runs under the whole upstairs. I turn on the bare lightbulb hanging from the ceiling. There are shadows everywhere from the support beams, the furnace pipes, and piles of junk and wobbly cardboard boxes stacked to the ceiling.

I imagine mutant hoarders peering at me from behind the furnace. Great. Now I have to circle it to prove I'm not a wuss.

I edge around a rusty stroller and scooch underneath the pipes to the farside, where I see a bolted door. I imagine there's a skull behind it and a bony hand sticking out of the ground. I take a deep breath, step over a box of china gnomes and a toy chest, and put my hand on the bolt.

*Come on, open it.*

But what if there *is* a skull behind it?

*Seriously?*

I throw the door open. On the other side there's a tiny room, all dark and dirty. Maybe it was a coal room.

My neck prickles. Someone's watching me from behind.

"Mom?"

Silence.

I turn around slowly. I can't see anyone. But someone's down here. I can feel it. "Who's there?"

There's a rustle in the coal room. I whirl back, bolt the door, and race for the stairs, tripping over a tricycle.

"Cameron?" Mom calls down from the kitchen. "Cameron, what are you doing down there?"

"Nothing."

Suddenly everything's normal again. The eyes staring at me? All in my head. The sound in the coal room? Maybe a mouse, maybe nothing.

Mom and C.B. come down the stairs to the basement. "Cameron, what did I say about wandering off? You know better."

*Nice, Mom. And you think I embarrass you?* "Sorry."

Mom registers the local dump. "Oh my." I can tell her fingers are itching for some hand sanitizer.

C.B. jumps right in: "I'll get Art to clear this out."

"Good."

C.B. chuckles. "He's a character. A confirmed bachelor. I expect some of this stuff has been here since his family got the place."

What, since the 1960s? I imagine the basement as a secret chamber of horrors.

"Cameron," Mom says, "there are two bedrooms upstairs. You can take your pick."

I roll my eyes. "So this really is going to be home?"

Mom nods. "It's got character."

*Right. For a creep house.*

# 4

My classes start today, Wednesday.

I hate first days. It's like all those nightmares where you're late for an exam and you can't find the classroom. Only on first days the nightmares are real. *Where is everything? Who is everybody? What am I doing here?* Worse, it's October, so everyone'll be in their cliques. Actually, around here, I'll bet they've been in their cliques since kindergarten.

The hardest part of first days, though, is keeping track of my lies. New kids get asked so many questions, but it's not like I can be honest, what with Mom being paranoid about Dad finding us. My name stays real so my school records can be transferred. Mom says that's okay because it's a common name and Dad has no access to my files. Everything else? Fake.

For starters, I have to remember what I've said about Dad. To keep it simple, I always start by saying Dad died, only then I get *How did he die? How did you feel? How old were you?* If I say he died a while ago, they want to know if I have a stepfather or if my mom has boyfriends. If I say recently, I have to remember not to smile or be happy for months.

It's weird pretending Dad's dead. If I pretend he's dead and he dies, will I feel guilty, like I made it happen?

Anyway, I pace at the foot of our lane, going over my story till the school bus arrives. Mom offered to drive me, but no way do I want to start off looking like a wimp.

Everyone's curious when I get on. The girls at the front try not to stare, but I hear them whisper after I've passed. I'll bet it's about the zit on my cheek. The guys in the back row give me attitude. The one in the middle looks pretty tough. I lower my head and make my way toward a couple of empty window seats. The kids on the aisle act like they don't see me. Maybe they're saving the seats for their friends. I end up alone a few rows ahead of the gang.

"Is he from Sinclair's dump?" the tough guy asks, loud enough for everyone to hear.

"Yeah," one of his friends says. "The dogs, Cody. Maybe he's dog food."

Cody laughs. "Yeah, he's dog food, all right."

Apparently this is funny.

Mom says if you ignore stuff, it'll go away. That's the stupidest advice in the world. Ignore stuff and it gets worse. Isn't that what she said about Dad? Anyway, what else can I do? I can hardly start something with a whole gang.

A chunky kid gets on at the next stop. All those free seats reserved for friends? Well, he isn't one of them either. He makes his way down the aisle while Cody and his gang make hog calls: "Sooey, sooey, here little piggy."

He slumps into the seat next to me smelling of stale sweat and breakfast cereal. I try to settle my nose on my hand without being obvious. "At least no one in my family is crazy," he mutters.

I don't say anything. He glances my way and blinks. "Hey, you're new."

*Actually I've been taking this bus since forever, only I have this super-power that makes me invisible.* "Yeah."

"I'm Benjie. Benjie Dalbert."

"Cameron Weaver." I check a fingernail and hope that's the end of our conversation. Cody and his gang are still making oink sounds. If they see me acting friendly, they could go after me again.

*Why am I such a coward?*

Coward? I don't even know the guy. Why should I be nice to him anyway? He stinks. Besides, I got called "dog food" and nobody said anything.

*Right. So I should act like everyone else?*

"So, where you from, Cam?" Benjie asks.

"Cameron. Boston." *Not.*

Benjie leans in. I can see bits of Cheerios between his teeth. "I have a cousin in Boston. So, like, what part?"

I try not to breathe. "It's more like a town outside Boston. I just say Boston because people have heard of it."

*Stop talking to me, Benjie. Please stop talking to me.*

"Yeah, but where?" He blinks. "Bedford?? Carlisle? My cousin's in Bedford."

"Carlisle."

"Cool." A spitball hits Benjie on the head. The gang laughs. Benjie turns round. "Quit it."

"Why, Piggy?" Cody taunts him. "You gonna do something about it, Piggy?"

Benjie's cheeks flush. "Jerks," he whispers. "They think they can run everybody. Cody Murphy, the biggest jerk? He deserves every bad thing that's ever happened to him. His mom gave him away, you know. Whenever he throws something at me, I remember that and I'm happy."

"His mom—what?"

"Gave him away. Great, huh?" Benjie blinks a couple more times. "He was eight or something. His dad died, and his mom remarried and shipped him from town to his grandparents here in the country."

"Harsh."

"Not harsh enough." Benjie grins. "Anyway, what are *you* doing here? I mean, you weren't born here. And it's not like any farms around Wolf Hollow are ever for sale. Did your folks split up? Are you staying with relatives?"

"Mom's rented a farmhouse." I look out the window.

"You're in Mr. Sinclair's old place?"

"Shh! Keep it down. Yeah. How do you know?"

"Because I've only lived here since forever, and it's the only house empty on the whole bus route. So, hey, is it haunted?"

I look back. "Haunted?"

"It should be," Benjie says. "He's weird."

"Who?"

"Sinclair. Who do you think? Don't ever get alone with him."

"How come?"

"He's got a sausage maker in his barn. You could end up in a meat pie."

"Gimme a break."

"It's what kids say. Anyway, I warned you."

Two girls get on the bus and sit at the front with their girlfriends. Cody's gang catcalls and snickers. For the rest of the ride, I watch the fields go by while Benjie goes on and on about the 4-H Club, which apparently stands for Head, Heart, Hands, Health and has fall fair competitions for teenagers and is really fun, and I should join, and his grandfather was the local leader till he got paralyzed by a stroke and ended up in the town nursing home. Blah, blah, blah. Anyway, it beats him asking me questions about my who, when, where, why.

The bus pulls into the parking lot. Benjie stays seated, eyes down, letting Cody's crew get off first. A couple of their gym bags "accidentally" bang against the side of his head. He pretends not to notice.

We're the last up the aisle. By the time we're out, Cody's gang is having a smoke at the side of the highway.

"Maybe I'll see you at lunch?" Benjie asks as we head in the front door.

"Sure, maybe." Great, something else to worry about—hurting his feelings or joining the loser crowd on the first day. As if I haven't already.

The morning's a blur of introductions in the office, guidance counseling, and my first two classes. There are way more kids here than I figured. Wolf Hollow may be a hiccup, but students are bused from all over the county. That's why it's built on the country side of the bridge to town.

At lunch I go into the cafeteria, concentrating on my guidance stuff so I can act like I don't see Benjie waving me over to a table with a bunch of other guys who look like they smell. I sit by myself in a corner, facing away from everyone, and pull a bagged sandwich and Coke out of my backpack.

The cafeteria's pretty loud. Chairs squeal as they're scraped over the cement tiles. Everyone yells over a bunch of announcements on the PA. And somewhere there's a kid with a laugh so shrieky you'd swear he was on helium. How long will I be putting up with this crap before Mom and I move again?

All of a sudden, Cody's gang crowds around me. He and a buddy plunk down on either side and stare, as if daring me to look at them. I do. Not for long, but enough to say I'm not afraid, which I am, and they know it.

"So, Cam," Cody says. "Is that your name? *Cam?*"

Cameron. "Sure."

"So, *Cam*, how come you're not with your pal Piggy?"

*I don't know. How come you're not with your mother?*

"Why would I be?" I say.

Cody's friends snicker.

"He stinks, huh?" Cody says, testing me.

"How would I know?"

"You sat beside him."

"He sat beside me."

"Either way. Or maybe you don't smell stink. Is that it? After all, you live in Sinclair's dump. Right, *Cam?*"

I force myself not to shake. "Why are you doing this?"

"Doing what?"

"Yeah, doing what?" the buddy on his right echoes.

"You know."

Cody puts his arm around my shoulder. "You're new. We're getting acquainted is all. I'm Cody. This here's Brandon, Mark, Stu, Dave. We're letting you know who's who, what's what."

"Yeah, okay," I nod, like that even makes sense.

"So anyway, *Cam*," Cody says real low, "what we want to know is…late at night, you hear the dogs?"

"What dogs?"

"You know. The *dogs*."

"I don't know." I swallow hard. "Tell me."

"Why? You scared, *Cam*?"

His buddies laugh, but not like anything's funny.

"No," I lie. "What's to be scared of?"

Cody squeezes my shoulder hard. "You live in Sinclair's dump. You'll find out." He gets to his feet and saunters out of the cafe. His buddies follow, laughing and barking.

Everyone's staring at me. Are they laughing too? I dump my trash in the garbage, lock myself in a bathroom stall down the hall, and rest my feet on the edge of the lid so no one will know I'm here.

Cody. The gang. I feel sick. But forget about them. What's the deal with Sinclair and the dogs?

*Nothing's the deal. Cody was just out to freak me out, to show me who's boss. That's what guys like him do.*

All the same…

# 5

My phone rings. It's Mom. "I caught you at lunch?"

"Yeah. Sort of."

"How's your first day?"

"Fine. Look, I'm kind of in the can."

Mom laughs. "I won't keep you then. This is just to say I may not be home when you get back. I'll be with Mr. Armstrong."

What's she doing with Cowboy Boots? "Are we moving someplace different?"

"No, no, nothing like that. Ken's offered to show me around town, that's all."

"*Ken?*" I roll my eyes. "He's a friend now?"

"Oh, for heaven's sake, Cameron, he's just being helpful. You never know who may be hiring, or when. Contacts can make all the difference. I should be home by five."

Sure enough, Mom's car's still gone when I get back. I go inside to watch some TV, but I get a better idea. With her away, it's the perfect time to go exploring. At our old place I snooped in her room to see if she had a gun or anything, what with Dad and all, but no, she's totally boring except for her pills. So instead I decide to go through the boxes in the basement. I've already inspected for psychos and mutants, so why not? The boxes won't be there long, and maybe I'll find something worth saving.

I slip downstairs into Shadowland. The air is cool like before. The cobwebs sag from the damp. If I listen to the silence, my mind'll start to play tricks, so I get to work. First I dig into the boxes of books. They're all romance novels and issues of *Farmers' Almanac*.

Next I go through the clothes boxes. There're trousers and long johns; some baby things—a boy's, I think, because they're blue; and a mess of wool sweaters full of brown rice. No, wait. That's not brown rice; that's mouse poop. I wipe my hands on my jeans and imagine what would have happened if I'd stuck them into a mouse nest.

I move on to the toy chest behind the furnace. Inside, I find more boys' stuff—a chewed-up hockey puck and a ratty baseball. There's also a yo-yo, a rubber ball attached to a paddle by an elastic string, a little mirror, a magnifying glass, and some marbles.

I wipe the dust off the magnifying glass and hold it in front of my hand. So there *was* a kid here, I think, examining my pores. Why didn't his family move his stuff when they sold the farm? I wonder what happened to him. He'd be as old as Grandpa. Weird.

"What are you up to?"

I whirl around. There's an old man hunched under the pipes staring at me. He's scrawny, with hair growing out of his nose and ears.

"Mom!" I scramble back.

"She's not here," he growls.

I glance at the stairs. If I try to escape, he'll block me. "Who are you? What are you doing here?"

"I own the place."

"You're Mr. Sinclair?"

He grunts. "You're the kid?"

He holds out his hand like I'm supposed to shake it. If I do, he could grab me. If I don't, I'll look like a coward.

I shake it. His hand is big and rough. For a second he doesn't let go. When he does, I fall back. He stares at me. *Mom, I need you.*

I try to swallow, but my throat's too dry. "How did you get in?"

"I have a key." He squints. "I knocked."

"I didn't hear you."

"Didn't hear me come down the stairs neither. You deaf or some-thing?" He pulls a handkerchief from his pocket. I picture him knocking me out with ether and dragging me to the meat grinder in his barn.

"What are you going to do?"

He horks into the handkerchief and puts it back in his pocket. "I'm going to clear out some of this junk is what I'm going to do. I hear your mother wants it gone."

"Where are the movers?"

"Why pay some fella to do what I can do myself?" Mr. Sinclair gets out from under the furnace pipes and hoists three boxes of books like they're nothing.

"There might be mice in those things," I say.

"Wouldn't be s'prised." He hauls the boxes up the stairs.

I feel kind of stupid standing around. "You want me to help?"

"If you've a mind to," he hollers without looking back.

For the next half hour I help him load the back of his pickup truck. He's a strange guy, like C.B. says. His face is all tanned and weather-beaten, but when he pulls off his cap to fan himself, his scalp is bald and pinky-white. Long gray strands from over his left ear are plastered across the top. Also, he clicks his tongue a lot.

"So, are there any dogs around here?" I ask as we head upstairs with some broken lawn chairs.

"Dogs? There's dogs most places."

"I know, but I mean… I don't know what I mean. It's just, at school, they said there were *dogs*. The way they said it, well…"

Mr. Sinclair kicks open the back shed door. "People say lots of things."

Mom's car drives up the lane. Mr. Sinclair goes over and introduces himself. When Mom looks at me, I can tell the first thing she sees is the dirt on my shirt.

"Your boy's been helping me clear that junk out of the basement," Mr. Sinclair says.

"Oh…good," Mom says. No way she can complain now.

"Got a good load here. There's more'n I remembered. I'll be back tomorrow or the next day for the rest."

"No rush," Mom says, but it's clear she wants it gone the day before yesterday. "Cameron, can you help me in with these groceries?"

I bring in three of the bags. While Mom starts dinner, I go back for the rest. Mr. Sinclair's about to leave.

"Mr. Sinclair, can I ask you something else?"

"You can ask. Doesn't mean I gotta answer."

I stick my hands in my pockets. "Did you know the boy?"

"What boy?"

"Didn't a boy live here before your father bought the farm? I guessed because of all the kid stuff in the basement. Not that it matters. It's just, I've moved around and had to leave a lot of things behind. That got me wondering why *his* things were left, and who he was and stuff."

Mr. Sinclair scratches his nose. "You wonder too much."

"That's what everyone says." I blush. "Anyway, I thought since you grew up on the next farm, maybe you'd know."

"Did you now?"

"Yes, and, well, do you?"

"You sure ask a lot of questions." Mr. Sinclair snorts a crusty chuckle, gets in his truck, and drives off.

# 6

Why didn't Mr. Sinclair answer? What's the big mystery?

*Who says there's a mystery? Maybe Mr. Sinclair didn't like the kid and just won't talk about him. Or maybe there wasn't a boy. Maybe the stuff is from when the owner was little and he went to a nursing home and it just got left.*

I think about maybes and what-ifs for I don't know how long, then go inside.

"Did you get lost?" Mom asks, laughing. She's already frying burgers and boiling mixed veggies. "Uh, about the rest of the groceries?"

"Sorry." This always happens when I think about things: my brain flies out the window. I go back to the car and bring in the last few bags.

Mom ladles out the food as I set the table. "So, how was your first day?"

"Great," I lie.

"Wonderful." Mom brings over our plates. "Could you give me some examples of what made it great?"

I sigh. "Great classes. Great locker. Great cafeteria."

"And the kids?"

"Great."

Mom waits for me to say something else, but I just start eating. She gives her amused smile, the one that says, *You're funny when you get like this*. "On the subject of great, I had a pretty great day myself."

"You made lots of contacts?"

"Even better. I got a job."

I practically choke. "What?"

"At least for now." Mom beams. "Ken's receptionist is having a baby. She's been working till he could find someone to take over. I said I had office experience, and, well, I'm shadowing her till the end of the week and taking over Monday."

"You'll be working for that real estate guy?"

"Don't frown. You'll give yourself wrinkles."

I slump into my chair. Cowboy Boots. Every day I'll be hearing about Cowboy Boots.

Mom reads my mind. "It's a job, Cameron. And he didn't ask for references."

References are a killer for Mom. She's scared that if a company checks her past, people at her old place will know where she's working now and Dad'll find out. Besides, who hires someone with a history of suddenly quitting?

"Terrific, then. Congratulations."

"Thanks." Mom's smile goes into overdrive. "I don't want to 'ruin your reputation,' but that offer of a ride to school is open. I can drop you off on my way to work and pick you up after five on my way home. You'd have time to join a club, finish your homework in the library."

Five? If I take the bus after school, that means I'll be here alone—and Mr. Sinclair has a key. But if Mom drives me, the gang on the bus will think I'm scared of them. I picture them crowding me at my locker: *Hey, Cammy, you scared, Cammy? Where's your mommy, Cammy?*

"The bus is good." I chew and swallow, but I don't taste anything. I'm underwater, hardly able to hear Mom when she asks me what's wrong. I stop eating and stare at my plate. Mom asks again.

"Nothing's wrong. Everything's fine. It's great."

Mom tilts her head. "Cameron, it's not. I can tell. What is it?"

I shrug. "There's nothing you can do."

"I can listen."

"Yeah, well, I don't have anything to say."

"Is it about my new job?"

"No. I'm glad about that. Really."

We sit for a while, not saying a word, then Mom clears my plate and brings me a bowl of ice cream for dessert. "Don't worry," she says quietly. "It'll get better. The first day at a new school is always hard. I remember when…"

I zone out while she tells me the story about what it was like for her when Grandpa and Grandma moved when she was little. One girl made her life miserable, but by the end of the year they were best friends. This story is supposed to let me know she understands what I'm going through, but it doesn't. It just makes me feel stupid, because apparently I don't know what I'm feeling. Also—*hello, Mom*—having a gang that can beat me up whenever it feels like it isn't like you having some girl who made fun of your sweater.

Besides, I'm not even thinking about school. I'm thinking about

Mr. Sinclair and whether I should tell Mom he has a key and he let himself into the house. I mean, he could do that in the middle of the night while we're sleeping. I picture him standing at the foot of my bed, staring at me.

*Stop it, that's crazy.*

Is it? Anyway, if I tell, so what? Mom'll freak, but then she'll say, "Every landlord has a key, and I *did* ask him to clear things out, so it's my fault. Don't worry. I'll talk to him about limits." And Mr. Sinclair'll say, "Sorry," and Mom will act like everything's fine. Only it won't be. Mr. Sinclair will know I'm scared, and he'll still have the key.

"...And by the end of the year, Marcia and I were best friends." Mom reaches across the table and puts her hand on mine. "Trust me, honey, things will get better. Things *always* get better."

"Oh yeah?" I pull my hand away, so mad I can't think. "Things always get better? Like with Dad?" Mom turns white. "I'm sorry. I didn't mean it."

Mom gets up and takes our dishes to the sink. She braces herself against the counter.

"Mom, I'm *sorry*. I'm really, really sorry."

"Never mind. Go do your homework."

"Mom—"

She raises her hand, not mad or anything, just like it's on a string. And I know that's it. Nothing I say can make it better.

# 7

I go up to my bedroom. It's at the top of the living room stairs, next to a small bathroom and near the big room over the kitchen. That's the room Mom thought I'd pick, and I would have, except for the trapdoor in the ceiling. It's sealed up with nails and paint. When I saw it, I asked Mom what she thought was up there.

"An attic."

"Yeah, but what's in it?" I pictured a dried-up body, half eaten by mice. I mean, who seals up an empty attic? Anyway, that's why I didn't choose the big room. If I don't see the hatch, it's easier not to think about what's on the other side.

The bedroom I picked came with an oak desk, a wooden chair, a night table with a lamp, and a metal-frame bed. The mattress is new, unlike the wallpaper, which is stained and peeling along the seams near the window. Under the peels are layers of older wallpaper, one with little orange canaries on it.

The window over my desk is the one good thing about my room. Looking out, I can see the barn with the fields all around and the woods in the distance. At night, the stars and the glow of the porch-lamp light up bits of the barn and the first row of cornstalks.

I start to do my homework. Pretty soon, though, I'm looking out the window, watching the stars come out and trying to forget my life. I wonder who all are staring up at the moon right now. Are they wondering the same thing?

Out of the corner of my eye, I catch something moving by the barn. When I look, it disappears. Wait. There it is again, at the cornfield. Some movement, some *thing*.

I count to twenty. Nothing. I relax. Then—did that stalk move? I turn off my light so whatever's out there can't see in.

*It's probably just a breeze.*

Or Mr. Sinclair. Or Cody and his gang.

*Don't be nuts. If it's anything, it's an animal. A coyote or a dog.*

The dogs. I close my curtains. If I don't look out, whatever's there will go away. But I can't *not* look. I sneak a peek. Nothing. *Wait. By the barn. Is that a boy?*

I blink. The boy is gone.

My eyes scan the barn. There's a missing board up in the loft area. The more I stare, the more I think I see the boy staring back at me from the shadows behind the hole. He's maybe ten, very pale, and he's wearing one of those old Davy Crockett hats with the raccoon tail hanging from the back. Are those freckles on his cheeks?

*Don't be crazy. The barn's too far away to see stuff like that.*

The face disappears. I stare till I see double. The face swims back into view.

This is too weird. I close my eyes and try to clear my head by thinking about the bus and the Cheerios between Benjie's teeth. When I open my eyes, everything's normal. There's no face. Nothing. Just the night.

And that's how it stays.

I close my curtains, get ready for bed, and crawl under the covers. I hate the way I scare myself. It's always the same and it's always stupid. And the scared-er I get, the more I talk to myself, which is even stupider.

Besides, even if there *was* a boy in the barn, what's scary about that? Maybe he just likes exploring places like I do. Still, it's weird he's on our property, especially so late. I wonder where he lives.

*Who says he lives anywhere? Who says he's real? What parents let a kid that young wander around at night?*

Mom knocks on my door. "Cameron?"

"Yeah?"

"May I come in?"

"Sure."

I know she wants to give me a good-night hug, but I told her to stop it when I was twelve, so she just stands in the doorway. "I know you didn't mean anything. You've had a hard day. I'm sorry I overreacted."

I hate it when she's all understanding. It makes me feel like an even bigger jerk. "That's okay. Mom, I really *am* sorry."

"I know." She pauses. "'Night, then. I love you."

I want to say the l-word back, but I feel dumb, so I just say, "You too."

Mom closes the door. I go to turn off my lamp and get flashes of Mr. Sinclair and the dogs and the kid I maybe saw in the barn. What's out there in the dark, circling the house when we're asleep? What *could* be out there?

I leave the light on.

# 8

Thursday is pretty much like Wednesday. I get on the bus and I take my place near the back, Cody's gang barking me down the aisle. A few minutes later, Benjie gets on and it's Oink City. I offer him a Tic Tac for his egg breath, but he doesn't take the hint. At lunch I hole up in the can and worry about everything. Then school's out and I'm back on the bus. I get off at the end of my lane.

It's cold and cloudy. The breeze makes it sound as if the corn-fields are whispering. I kick a stone up the lane. Past the stalks, I see Mr. Sinclair's truck poking out from behind the house. He must be clearing the rest of the garbage.

I don't exactly feel like being alone with him again, so I slip into the cornfield and follow the rows along the yard and down the side of the house till I reach the rail fence by the barn. I'm totally hidden, but I can see out between the stalks like a spy.

The shed door at the back of the house swings open. Mr. Sinclair comes out with some boxes. He carries them to his pickup, tosses them on the cargo bed, and goes back inside.

Corn tassels tickle my nose; leaves wave in front of my face. I need a better lookout. I glance at the barn. That hole up where I thought I saw the kid would be perfect. I break from the field, hop the fence, and sprint to the barn. It's dark inside except for a few shafts of light from the cracks between the boards. There are wooden stairs ahead on a concrete pad set on the dirt floor. I can also make out cow stalls.

I climb to the hayloft, testing each step in case it's loose or rotten. It's empty except for an overturned pail and the birds lining the rafters. Where there's birds, there's bird crap. Guess I won't be sitting down.

I crouch by the hole. There's no sign of Mr. Sinclair. He must still be inside. I glance at my bedroom window. If my curtains were open, I could see right in. I picture night stalkers lurking around up here, watching me.

The curtains move. Mr. Sinclair's the only one in the house. What's he doing in my room?

Mr. Sinclair comes out of the shed with two cartons. That's impossible. He can't be outside and in my room at the same time. Then who's there? Mr. Sinclair heaves the cartons in the cargo bed, gets in his truck, and starts the engine.

"Mr. Sinclair! Wait! Don't leave. There's someone in my room!"

Not hearing me, he drives to the lane. I barrel down and race to the door. Too late. He's gone. What do I do now? I pull out my phone to call Mom.

*Wait. If I tell her a stranger's in the house, she'll call the police—and what if I'm wrong? Maybe I just saw a cloud shadow cross the window.*

But what if I'm right?

*Calm down. I'm scaring myself for nothing. Who'd be inside? One look at this dump and a thief would know there's nothing to steal.*

*And what random guy's going to break into a house in the middle of nowhere?*

What if the guy isn't random? What if it's Dad? He could've parked at the next crossroad and walked back easily.

*Stop thinking like Mom.*

Why? There's always news about some guy who goes nuts and kills his family.

*Dad wouldn't do that. Would he?*

I try to think of everything and anything except the last night we lived together. No use.

I was eight. It was after supper. I can't remember how it started, but Mom and Dad were fighting again. Their fighting was supposed to be a secret. There were lots of secrets with Dad. Like the secret about him teaching me how to swim and holding my head underwater till I thought I was drowning. "It's training, Buddy."

This last fight, Dad started smashing stuff.

"Not in front of Cameron," Mom said.

I ran upstairs like I always did, hid under the covers, stuck my fingers in my ears, and prayed I wouldn't wet the bed like I used to do when they'd fight. I'd be so ashamed. "Don't tell Dad," I'd say, and Mom would hug me and promise.

Anyway, the fight was so bad I could still hear them. Dad yelled the kind of stuff he always did: "Who is it? What's his name?"

"There is no 'he.' There's nobody," Mom yelled back.

"You think I'm stupid? It's that guy at the drugstore, isn't it? Don't lie to me. I've seen the way you look at each other. I know."

The screaming went on and on. I sang songs to myself to block it out, and then the police came. They drove me to a shelter where a woman put me in a room and gave me a teddy. I was way too old for it, but I didn't care.

"Where's Mom?" I asked. "Where's Dad?"

All they said was, "Your mom's okay." Someone kept checking in on me until Grandma and Grandpa arrived the next day.

"Don't worry," Grandma said. "We love you. Everything's fine." They said Mom had had an accident and was in the hospital, and Dad was away on business. Then they took me to an apartment where we stayed for a month till Mom got better. They wouldn't let me see her. When I asked why not, Grandma would tear up and leave the room.

"When's Dad getting back?" I'd ask, and when I was braver: "Why were there police?"

"Let's not think about that," Grandpa said. "Let's think happy thoughts."

But at night, when they thought I was asleep, I heard Grandma say, "He's a monster. She can't go back. Next time she could be dead."

Next time. Were there other times? When? Was it on those days Mom stayed in bed with the lights off? She'd say she had a head-ache or the flu. Dad was always nice those days. He'd bring home flowers and toys and order in pizza or Chinese takeout, and we'd watch TV together.

I never saw Dad again, except on supervised visits at that govern-ment building. I remember the blue walls and the plate of cookies and the cameras and the social worker in the corner.

I was scared seeing him at first. I figured there must be a reason we couldn't be alone, but he was always gentle, and when I'd back away from him, his face would crumple up and I'd feel mean. I remember when I finally let him lift me onto his lap. He put his arm around me, and I cried into his shoulder. I didn't care who saw.

Dad rocked me. "It's okay, Buddy. Don't be scared. Sometimes people say things about other people that aren't true. Just so you know, I love you and your mom, and I'd never do anything bad to either of you."

"But what about that night?"

"Sometimes your mother did things behind my back and we'd get mad at each other. That night, she was so mad she stormed up the stairs, tripped, and fell. She hurt herself by accident, promise."

"Then why aren't we together?"

Dad got very quiet. "Your grandma and grandpa don't like me. They say all kinds of things, don't they, Buddy? You know how people can put ideas in other people's heads?"

I nodded.

He tousled my hair. "Here's something else. Since that night I haven't had a drink. Not one. You can tell your mom. Maybe she won't believe me, but it's true."

I remember my last visit with Dad, before Mom and I started running. Dad had this weird look in his eyes. He waited till the social worker's back was turned. Then he slipped me a photo of him and me at the beach.

"Don't let anyone see this," he whispered. "Your mom would take it away. She doesn't want you thinking about any of the good times we had. But you and me, we remember, don't we, Buddy?"

"Sure."

"Shh. My new address and cell number are on the back. Our secret? Cross your heart and hope to die?"

I nodded and slipped the photo into my pocket. I was scared about hiding it, but Dad was right. Mom would be mad if she saw it. Back home, I put it behind the picture of Mom and me with my grandparents that sits on my bedside table.

The weird thing is, I've never looked at the photo since. I'm afraid if I take it out I'll see Dad's number and have this overwhelming need to call him. And I can't. Not ever. I've thought of getting rid of it so I won't get tempted, but I can't do that either. What if I want it someday to remember what he looked like? So there it is beside my bed, the secret photo: Dad, hidden out of sight but always on my mind, like in life.

After I put the photo in my pocket, Dad hugged me for the last time. "I love you. I love your mom too. If I didn't love her so much, the things she did wouldn't have made me so mad. Trust me: there are things you'll know when you're older."

That's exactly what Mom says: "There are things you'll know when you're older." Well, guess what? I can't wait till I'm older. There's things I need to know *now*.

# 9

I peek through the hole in the barn wall and stare at the house. Dad *couldn't* have stalked us here already.

*Oh yeah? When we split, he might have been parked around the corner. Or hired a detective. Or slipped a GPS chip under Mom's car at the mall or at work.*

No, I'm just scaring myself. Dad's far away, all lonely and missing me, not knowing where I am. Maybe. I just have to go inside and prove it.

*Don't be stupid. Remember those movies where the babysitter hears something in the attic and checks it out? Everyone always says, "That's crazy, who'd ever do that?"*

This is different. If there's nobody there, I won't have scared Mom for nothing. And if it *is* Dad, well, *then* I can warn Mom. I have a phone, after all. Besides, I'm not in danger; he never did anything to me.

*He did.*

Not much and hardly *ever*, and maybe I dreamed it. Anyway, I have to do this. For Mom.

I walk to the house, eyes forward, shoulders back like I'm not afraid of anything. I open the back door and step inside.

"Hello," I call out super loud. "Is anybody there?"

Silence.

"If anybody's there, I live here, okay? So I'm going to walk through the house now. If you're a thief or something, I'll be going up the living room stairs, so you can run down from the big room and escape through the kitchen and I won't even see you. Okay?"

*Great. I sound like a dork.*

I go from the kitchen through the downstairs bathroom into Mom's room. I look under her bed—nobody—and in her closet—nobody. I stick my head into the living room—nobody—and stand at the foot of the stairs.

"This is your last chance," I shout. "If you don't go now, Mom'll be here any minute, and I have a phone so you better not try anything. I mean it. Okay? Fine. Don't say I didn't warn you. Here I come!"

I climb the stairs, look in the small bathroom—nobody—and inspect my bedroom—nobody. I pause at the door to the big room over the kitchen, then throw it open. The room's empty; the trap-door to the attic is sealed as always. The only thing left to check is the basement.

I go back down to the kitchen. The door to the basement is open. Was it open when I came in? I can't remember. But hey, who'd leave the door open if they were trying to hide?

*The only way to know is to go down.*

I get a flashlight from the drawer to the right of the sink. It's hardly a great weapon, but at least it's something if anyone tries to jump me. Also, I won't have to worry about the overhead light going out, like in those movies.

I flick the light switch. "Dad? Dad, are you down there? If you are, please let me know, because you're scaring me. Also, because I want to see you. I've missed you."

Silence.

I remember when I was two or three. Dad drove me out to the middle of nowhere, a forest or something. No one was around and he hid behind a tree. I thought he'd left me, abandoned me with no one anywhere. I didn't know what to do. I cried and cried. Dad watched the whole time. He thought it was funny.

The stairwell looks more like a tomb than ever. I try to stay calm by counting to ten over and over. Before I know it, I'm at the bottom.

The place is cleared out except for the furnace. Once I circle it, I'll know everything's okay. I duck under the pipes real fast so if anyone's hiding, they won't have time to run around and get me from behind.

There's nobody there.

*What about inside the coal room?*

I stare at the little door. "Dad?"

Silence.

I turn on the flashlight, throw open the door, and jump back like I'm expecting something to pop out. Nothing does. I shine the light inside. Except for some pieces of coal in the corners, it's empty. Mission accomplished. Home secure. Phantom army destroyed.

I'm about to close the door when I see something scratched on the left wall. I lean in for a better look. There's three groups of four short lines with a fifth line crossing them, plus two extra lines.

*Was somebody locked in here, counting days?*

I wipe my forehead with the back of my hand. My light hits a dusty cardboard folder propped against the inside wall to the left of the door. No wonder I didn't see it before. Who would? It could've been hidden here since forever.

I pick it up and smell mold. A chill shoots through my body. I imagine corpse fingers squeezing my bones. I run up to the kitchen and everything's fine again—except my hands are smudged with soot from the folder. When Mom sees the tiniest bit of dirt on my shoes, she goes wacko: "You're tracking *mud* through the *whole house!*" If I spread coal dust, I'll be dead.

I put the folder in a plastic bag from under the sink and wash my hands. Then I grab some paper towels and take the bag up to my room. After I cover my desk with the towels, I open the folder flap and pull out the stuff inside. There's a pile of kids' drawings, some crayon and pencil stubs, and a black-and-white wedding photo in a cardboard frame.

The bride and groom have strange, dead eyes. On the back, there's fancy handwriting:

*Mr. and Mrs. Frank McTavish. May the Lord bless thee and keep thee. May the Lord be gracious unto thee. May the Lord lift up the light of His countenance upon thee and give thee peace.*

*August 1, 1948*

Someone else has put an arrow beside "Mrs. Frank McTavish" and written "Evelyn née Cartwright."

At the bottom, a kid has printed "Mother and Father." He must be the boy who made the drawings and whose things were in the basement. He's printed his first name in the bottom right corner of all the pictures: "Jacky." So he's Jacky McTavish.

The top drawings are mostly of Jacky and his mother and father at the farm. His father is huge—even bigger than the barn. He has enormous black eyes, without any whites, and a mouth of yellow teeth. Plus he almost always has a pitchfork, a hammer, or a saw. Jacky and his mother are way smaller and mostly off to the side holding hands. Her eyes are empty circles; sometimes she doesn't have a mouth.

But what give me goose bumps are the pictures of Jacky. He's wearing a Davy Crockett cap.

*He was the kid in the barn last night.*

No. There was no kid in the barn last night. If there was, I imagined the cap. It was too dark to see.

*Really?*

Really. Anyway, if a kid with a Davy Crockett cap was trespassing last night, it wasn't this kid. He'd be old by now.

I concentrate on the drawings. Mixed in with the family pictures are a few drawings of two boys climbing trees and playing on boulders in the middle of a clearing. I'll bet they're in the woods at the back of the field. I recognize Jacky because of the cap, but who's the other one?

*Mr. Sinclair?*

That would make sense; he lived on the next farm over.

*But if Mr. Sinclair played with Jacky, why won't he talk about him?*

Questions, questions. If I'm not careful, I'll be as paranoid as Mom.

I work my way through the rest of the pile. Jacky's mother's disappeared. Jacky's father was still around though. In some drawings, lightning shoots out of his head, like in comics where some crazy super-villain's going nuts. In others, he holds Jacky over his head with one hand like he's a doll. Jacky's hands are in the air. It's hard to tell if he's waving or trying to get help.

Finally I get to the drawings at the bottom of the pile. My heart stops.

Dogs. Packs of dogs. Their teeth are jagged. Their tails are like whips. And everywhere there's scribbles of purple and black and red.

# 10

om brings home KFC. Over dinner I ask her how things
went at C.B.'s office and try hard to stay interested. Mostly,
though, I think about Jacky's drawings.

The dogs. What happened to them? Why did Cody ask if I heard
dogs at night? He couldn't have meant *them*, could he? Those drawings are fifty years old.

And what about Jacky? Why did he stop drawing his mother? Did
something happen to her? And what's with his father's pitchfork,
his hammer, his eyes? I think about him holding Jacky up with
one hand—and suddenly remember Dad swinging me around in
circles when I was little. Mom's screaming at him to put me down.
Now we're on the balcony and Dad's dangling me by a leg over the
railing. "Shut up. You wanna see him fly?"

After dinner I go to my room and look at the drawings again. I
start seeing random arms, legs, and heads in the scribbles around
the dogs. I get into bed and turn out the lights.

After forever, I fall asleep…

I'm in the cornfield. It's night and I'm running. The dogs are
after me. Paws pound the earth. Barks fill the air. They're getting
closer. I fall down, get up, fall down again. Cornstalks snap behind
me. They're going to get me. *Help!*

"They won't hurt you. I won't let them." It's a boy. Where?

I blink and I'm in my room under the covers in the dark. I'm sweating. My heart's pounding.

I feel a draft. Something's in the room. Someone.

"Mom?"

Silence. I try to move. I can't.

"Who's there?"

*It's me. Jacky.*

I didn't hear that. That was just me talking to myself.

*Don't be scared.*

"I'm not scared. You're a voice in my head. That's all you are."

*No. I'm Jacky. I'm glad you're here. I've been lonely since Mother and Father left.*

"Stop it. Leave me alone. I'm Cameron, Cameron Weaver. Whatever you are, you're not real."

"Why are you being like that?" Jacky's voice—it's not in my head anymore. It's in the room.

I panic. "I'm still dreaming. That's it. I dreamed I woke up from a nightmare, only I went into another nightmare, this one. Well, now I'm going to wake up for real."

"What are you talking about?"

"Wake up!" I yell. "Wake up!"

"Don't shout," Jacky says. "You'll worry your mother."

Oh no—I'm still here, wherever here is. How do I wake up?

"I thought you'd like me. I thought we'd be friends."

*"Help!"*

"Don't you like me?"

*"Wake up! Help!"* I try to grab at the lamp on my night table, but I'm tangled in bedsheets, wrapped up like a mummy. *"Wake up! Help!"*

Mom turns on the light. "Cameron?"

I can't say anything. I'm panting, freezing, boiling. I look to the desk. There's nothing there. I look at the closet. It's closed. Is he inside? No—there's nothing inside. I've had a dream, that's all. But if I've had a dream, why doesn't this feel like waking up?

Mom sits at the edge of my bed. "You're soaking wet." She feels my forehead. "You have a fever. Let me get you something."

"No. Don't go."

"Everything's fine."

"It's not."

"It will be." She smoothes my hair off my forehead. "I'll be right back."

"Mom—"

Mom opens my closet door. "There's nothing in the closet," she says gently. "There's nothing under the bed either."

"I know that. I'm not a baby."

"I know." Mom comes back to my bed. "Cameron, these fears of yours, they're not your fault. It's your father. Every time we move, the nightmares come back. But they go away. They always have. They will this time too. Remember that." She gives me a kiss on the forehead and goes to get stuff from the bathroom.

Mom's right. It always starts like this in a new place. The nightmares come, but worst of all, they never feel like nightmares. They feel real. I see something like the kids' stuff in the basement, and I start imagining things. Next thing you know, I'm on Planet Psych Ward.

Mom comes back in a minute, sticks a thermometer in my mouth, and pats my face with a cool cloth. She checks my temperature. "Like I thought, a fever." She gives me some medicine and has me bundle myself in a blanket while she changes my sheets. I'd help but I'm shivering too much.

"All right then," Mom says. "Back into bed." She tucks the covers under my chin. "You're staying home from school tomorrow."

*What? I'll be here alone all day? With Sinclair next door and nightmares whenever I close my eyes?*

Mom reads my mind. "Don't worry, I'll stay home too. I'll tell Ken you're sick."

"No, don't embarrass me. I'll be fine!"

"You're sure?"

"Of course I'm sure." *Not.*

She gives me a close look. "All right then. But do me a favor: no zombie games. They don't help."

# 11

I wake up Friday feeling as cold and gray as the sky. Mom brings me oatmeal and toast on a tray and leaves me a sandwich and an apple for lunch, plus a pitcher of water. She's really nice when I'm sick.

"Call me if there's a problem. I'll be back no later than five," she says.

Being sick is boring. I always think I'll have fun watching TV and playing video games, but after a couple of hours I want to be doing stuff. Sometimes I sneak out, but not today. I don't feel like throwing up or anything, but every time I move, I get chills.

After breakfast I pick up my tablet and check out old friends on Facebook. I'm super careful. Mom told me about privacy settings when we first ran away. She said she didn't want me to have an FB account, but sooner or later she knew I'd get one anyway. Telling me now was like Grandma and Grandpa telling her about birth control: "You need to know how to protect yourself so you'll be ready when the time comes." I guess I wasn't paying attention because she grabbed me by the shoulders. "This is important, Cameron. If you don't pay attention, your father can get into your account and figure out where we are, and we could end up dead. Understand?"

When I turned ten I lied about my age and got my account, using a fake name and a picture of a sci-fi mutant for my profile. I made sure no one could see my page except friends I approved, then I searched for kids I used to play with. A few had secret accounts like mine, a few others supervised by parents. I messaged about why I'd left and told them to call me "Rob Booker" online. Because I had an alias, I thought I could talk about everything.

Only somebody—a.k.a. Dad—went creeping. He created a fake Cameron Weaver account and sent friend requests to kids he knew I'd played with.

Tommy Gee, the idiot, clicked Accept and messaged: "Using your real name again, 'Rob'?"

And "Cameron Weaver" said, "Yeah, LOL."

Tommy asked, "You coming back from Wellington?"

When I found out, I told Mom and we were on the run again.

For a while, friends posted "Good luck, Rob" on their time lines, and messages piled up in my inbox, but I was too scared to write back, except to tell Tommy he'd ruined my life.

I promised Mom I'd never use Facebook again. I haven't either, except to see what my old friends are doing. Like, Tony is on the junior football team, which is funny because he used to be smaller than everyone else. And Laurie, who was my "girlfriend" because we held hands for maybe a second, is dating some guy I've never heard of. None of them mentions me anymore. Maybe they're scared to get me in trouble again. Or maybe they've just moved on. Either way, it sucks. It's like I don't exist. Like I'm a ghost.

That's why I don't check much. Besides, reading their thoughts makes me feel like a stalker, and that makes me think of Dad. Am I turning into him? I should quit checking forever. Who needs friends anyway?

I remember when Mom told me we'd never be going home again.

"But what about Tommy and Tony and everyone?" I cried.

"You'll make new friends," Mom said.

Right. Only whenever I do, we move again and the hurt just gets bigger. It's better not to have friends. If I need to talk to someone, I should just talk to myself. At least that's something I'm good at it.

I put my tablet to sleep, close my eyes, and float to that place where I know I'm dreaming but I also know it's daytime and I'm safe in my room. That's why I'm not worried when I hear Jacky's whisper: "I'm sorry I scared you last night." He sounds pretty fragile.

"That's okay." I'm not sure if I mumble this or if I just think it.

"It's no fun being alone."

"No fun at all."

"I've been alone since Father went away."

I picture him sitting cross-legged on my desk. He looks like the kid I thought I saw in the barn, very small and pale, with light freckles on his nose. And he has that cap with the raccoon tail and clothes like in old movies.

My eyelids flicker. When they're open, Jacky's gone. When they're closed, he's there again. So I'm just dozing. Good. I sink back into my drift. Jacky is fiddling with the tail of his cap.

"Where did your father go?" I ask, half bored.

Jacky looks at his shoes. "I don't know. He was with the dogs. Where's *your* father?"

"Probably back where we left him."

Jacky frowns. "Did he cry when you left?"

"Maybe. I don't know."

"Father never cried."

"Why do you call him Father? Why not Dad or Daddy?"

"Because. He's Father, that's all. You ask weird questions." He scrunches his nose. "Cameron…does your mother have a friend?"

"She has lots of friends. *Had* lots of friends."

"I don't mean a friend. I mean a *friend*."

"A man friend?"

Jacky nods.

I remember Mom's fights with Dad and the things he said. "I don't know. I don't think so." And I sure don't want to think about it.

"Mine does," Jacky whispers. "Father said she'd still be with us if it weren't for him. After she left, he got the dogs. To keep bad people away, people who'd take me."

"The dogs in your drawings?"

"They're everywhere. Even when you can't see them. If you're not careful, they'll get in the house."

I sit up, wide awake. There's a draft from the window. I pull my blanket up around me and look outside. Clouds blow across the sky. I hear dogs howling in the wind. Correction: I hear a sound *like* dogs howling in the wind. Because there *aren't* any dogs, just my mind playing tricks. Jacky's dogs are long dead. And the real Jacky isn't a kid anymore; he's Mr. Sinclair's age.

*If he's alive.*

Why wouldn't he be?

*People die. Maybe Jacky's a ghost.*

Get real.

*Look, if Jacky died when he was a kid, he'd look like what I saw: small, pale, with those old-fashioned clothes and that stupid cap. Right?*

Wrong. I don't know what Jacky looked like. I've only seen him in crayon drawings.

*Unless I saw his ghost.*

Stop thinking like that.

*Fine. Stopping now. But—*

I pick up my tablet and start a game of Zombie Attack. Jacky, a ghost? That's dumber than imagining mutant hoarders in the basement or Dad in my room.

My screen fills up with the walking dead. They pop out of manholes and lurch out of alleys faster than I can use my flamethrower. I lose three lives in two minutes and have to start over. Next game I get to the abandoned homestead but forget about the zombie hiding in the freezer and the ones behind the couch. What's wrong with me? I'm usually good at this.

I put down my tablet. Jacky can't be a ghost. He doesn't even look sick.

*What if he had an accident? Say he fell out of that hole in the barn and broke his neck.*

Then I'd be seeing him with his head on backward.

*Or got run down by a corn harvester.*

He'd be full of holes.

*Or the dogs killed him.*

He'd be covered in teeth marks.

*Okay then, what if he was murdered?*

Murdered?

*Yeah. What if his father murdered him? It's not hard to imagine. Remember the drawings? The hammer, the pitchfork, the way his dad grabbed him?*

No. The Jacky in my dream said his father went away. That means he'd have been alive after his father left.

*Not if he was murdered. He'd have seen his father leave, but his ghost would have stayed behind.*

I'd better shut up or I'll drive myself crazy.

*What if I already am?*

# 12

**M**om says the best way to stay cool is to be prepared, and the best way to be prepared is to know the facts. I spend the rest of the day googling.

"Wolf Hollow + dogs" turns up lots of hits, but they're all for vets or puppies for sale. The words "Wolf Hollow + murder" turn up stories about a local couple who were killed on vacation in Mexico in 2005. I do a bunch of combinations that include other search words like "Sinclair" and "1960s" and get a link to a Wally Sinclair who used to be an councilman. Other than that, nothing. What a relief.

By the time Mom comes home, I've settled down. It's what always happens. I drive myself bananas over nothing, then out of nowhere, the pressure pops like a blister. Then I'm calm till I think about something else and the pressure starts to build again. That usually happens right away, like now, as I head downstairs for dinner.

*It doesn't matter if a Google search came up empty. Big-city newspapers put their old stories online, but local papers in small towns? Recent stuff maybe, but anything from way back would be in storage somewhere.*

The only way for me to stop thinking like a lunatic is to know for sure what happened to Jacky. But how? I can just picture me walking up to the lady at the front desk of the town newspaper, the *Weekly Bugle*.

**Me**: Hi. Did your paper ever publish any stories about a kid being murdered on the farm where I'm living?

**Receptionist**: A murder? When?

**Me**: I don't know. Maybe half a century ago?

**Receptionist** (rolling her eyes): Can you be more specific?

**Me**: Not really.

**Receptionist**: Who was murdered?

**Me**: A kid called Jacky McTavish, but I'm not *sure* he was murdered.

**Receptionist** (eyeballs bouncing off the ceiling): Let me get this straight—you want the *Bugle* to rummage around for stories that were possibly published over half a century ago about a murder that may or may not have happened?

**Me**: Yes, please.

**Receptionist**: And, if I may ask, why do you think there might have been a murder?

**Me**: Because it would explain the ghost.

**Receptionist**: The ghost?

**Me**: Yes, I saw a ghost. Or maybe I just had a dream. And by the way, could you also check for stories about wild dogs?

**Receptionist**: Young man, does your mother know you're here?

I sit down at the table. Mom's made an omelet, with mashed potatoes and peas on the side.

"You're looking much better," she says.

"Thanks. I feel better too." I don't feel like eating, but I don't want Mom to think I'm still sick and make me stay home to get creeped out again, so I have a bite. Out of nowhere, I get an inspiration for how to find out about the murder!

"So, Mom," I say, "would the real estate office know about the farms around here? Like, who's bought and sold them from the beginning?"

"No, but it'd be easy to find out. Property records are at the registry office next to the town hall."

"Good. Would they say if there was anything unusual about a farm?"

"Well, if there were termites, I guess. Or asbestos in the insulation."

"But other things?"

"Like?"

"I don't know. Deaths maybe?"

Mom gives me a close look. "In cities, deaths are sometimes mentioned in case a buyer is superstitious. But out in the country, people liked to die at home. It was so common that they probably wouldn't mention it."

I doodle in my mashed potatoes with my fork. "What if someone was murdered?"

"They might mention that."

"Great. So can I ask you a favor? If you have time tomorrow, could you please check into this place?"

"Here?" Mom chews slowly. "Why?"

"Because people at a registry office won't want to be bugged by a kid."

"Cameron, is your imagination acting up again?"

"No." I want to leave it at that, but Mom's not stupid. "It's for a history project. My teacher wants us to research something local and write about what it means to us. Because I'm new, he said I could write the history of what brought me here."

She puts down her knife and fork, alarmed.

"Don't worry," I say quickly. "I knew you wouldn't like that, what with Dad and all. So I suggested I write about the history of the farm instead. I told my teacher it means something to me because since I'm living here, I'm part of its history from now on. Like, I'm its next chapter."

Mom smiles. "I'll bet he liked that."

"Uh-huh." I nod, all serious, like I'm gunning for an A. "And I thought if there was something juicy, like a murder or a suicide, it'd make my essay way more interesting. I know there probably isn't. All the same, I'm kind of hoping."

Mom looks amused. "Okay, I'll find out what I can. Maybe not tomorrow, but in the next few days. Don't be disappointed when everything comes back normal."

I hate being sneaky, but I have to say I'm pretty good at it. I fill my face with mashed potatoes.

"Also, don't expect me to do your homework," she adds. "If I find you the names of the people who owned the farm, the dates it was bought and sold, and anything unusual that might come up—like a murder or a suicide—you have to promise to do some research of your own. Interview Mr. Sinclair. I'm sure he knows lots about what's gone on around here."

The mashed potatoes stick to my throat. "What if he won't say?"

"Don't be silly. What would he have to hide?"

*Oh, things about a murder maybe.*

"Who knows? It's just, I already asked him some stuff when he was cleaning out the basement, and he got all weird."

Mom laughs. "He is a bit gruff, isn't he? Don't take it personally. He was probably just in a hurry to get the job done. If it makes you feel awkward, I'll make the call for you." Before I can stop her, she goes to the phone and dials.

"Mr. Sinclair? It's Katherine Weaver… No, no problems, everything's great. The students at Cameron's school are doing a local-history project. He was wondering if he could talk to you about the farm some time. How people cleared the land, harvested, socialized, that sort of thing. He's got the flu at the moment, so this weekend's not so good, but maybe at the beginning of the week."

*Please say no.*

"Thanks. I'll tell him. Bye for now." She hangs up, beaming. "You can go over to Mr. Sinclair's Monday evening after supper."

Me and my big mouth.

# 13

Sunday afternoon, I do my weekly happy call with Grandma and Grandpa, but by Monday morning I'm feeling good for real. Jacky, or whatever that ghost thing was, hasn't shown up again, so he was probably just in my head on account of my fever. At least I hope so.

Outside, there's a light frost. I stomp my feet to keep warm while I wait for the bus and watch the farmer across the road harvesting his corn. I can't wait for Mr. Sinclair to do the same. Once the fields are cleared, I can stop imagining the cornstalks as a hiding place for night stalkers, bullies, and dogs.

The bus arrives. I take a deep breath and get on, prepared for Cody's gang to start barking. Instead they talk about me so loudly that I can hear them from the front of the bus.

"Look who's back. Dog Food," Cody's buddy Dave says. "Looks like Dog Food didn't get eaten after all." *Ha-ha, very funny.*

"Dog Food?" Cody grins. "He's more like Chicken Feed." *Brack-brack* chicken sounds come from his crew.

"I was sick," I call back.

"Aww. Cammy was sick."

I want to sit far away from them, but that'd only prove I'm a coward. Besides, the kids on the aisle saving the window seats want me away from them like I wanted away from Benjie.

The gang clucks me to my seat, where I close my eyes and wait for it to be Benjie's turn. When he slumps beside me, he asks where I was Friday. I tell him and he blinks. "Hey, don't breathe on me. I don't want to catch your germs."

*Worry about your own breath. It could kill the whole school.*

As the bus pulls into the parking lot, I get up the nerve to say, "Benjie, something's bothering me. My first day on the bus, you asked if my place was haunted. Why? Was there a murder there?"

"No." He laughs. "I asked on account of the dogs."

"What dogs?"

"You know—*the dogs*. It's why Cody barks at you."

"What are you talking about?"

Benjie blinks. "Years ago, the farmer at your place got killed by his dogs."

"Seriously?"

Benjie grins. "Cool, huh? Ripped apart and eaten! Ask anyone. The story's famous around here."

The door opens. Cody's gang pushes up the aisle. Benjie hunkers in till they're past us.

"They say when the wind's up, you can hear them," he says as we grab our backpacks and follow everyone out. "Some parents tell their kids if they're bad, the dogs will get them. But everybody knows that if you hear something, it's just coyotes."

I relax. "So you asked because of the dogs, not because of a murder."

"Are you kidding? Nobody gets murdered around here. We're too boring." He looks over at Cody's gang on the side of the road. "Don't say that to Cody though."

"Don't say what? That the town is boring?"

"No, that there wasn't a murder on your farm."

"Why not?"

"Just don't."

Cody looks our way. Benjie takes off.

I wish Benjie hadn't added that last part. Why does Cody think there was a murder? How can I talk to him about it without him going mental on me?

I think about that all day. At dinner I hardly hear anything Mom says except, "It's time for you to head over to Mr. Sinclair's."

I put on my lined jacket.

"Where are your gloves? And your hat?"

"Mom."

"We're nearing the end of October. It's cold and you've been sick."

"I'll hardly be out that late."

"Cameron, it's already getting dark. Which reminds me—give me a call when you're done, and I'll drive over to pick you up."

"What? I'll just be one farm over."

"There are no streetlights. It'll be hard to see."

"Mom, stop!"

Mom sighs. "Fine. At least take this flashlight." She fishes it from the drawer, and I slide it into my jacket pocket. "And don't forget to walk on the left side of the road, facing traffic."

"Yeah, like I'm too stupid to know that." Actually I would've forgotten.

By the time I head out, Mom has me bundled up like I'm on an Arctic expedition. I take off my hat and gloves as soon as I'm down the lane, but it really *is* cold. I put them back on again and walk fast to keep from freezing. The neighbor on the other side has harvested half his field. It's like it's had a buzz cut; you can see forever. I try to forget what could be hiding in Sinclair's fields to my right and speed up even more.

Mr. Sinclair's place is nicer than ours. The potholes in his lane are filled with gravel, and the house is yellow brick instead of tar paper. There's something strange though. All the curtains are closed and I don't see any lights, except for a lamp on the porch and one out at the barn.

I head up the stone walkway to the front door. How will I get Mr. Sinclair to talk about Jacky and his family? How do I ask if Jacky got murdered?

I bang the heavy brass knocker three times. Silence.

*Remember Benjie's story about Sinclair's meat grinder and ending up in a meat pie?*

Don't be stupid. Mom knows where I am. Sinclair can't do anything to me without getting caught.

*Unless he kills Mom right after.*

Yeah, like that's going to happen, except in a movie. I bang the door again. Nothing.

The only light left in the sky is deep purple to the west. I take out my flashlight and go around to the back of the house, pressing my face against the windows and shooting the beam through the cracks between the curtains. Inside is a clutter of sofas and knickknacks.

So where's Mr. Sinclair? He knows I'm coming.

*What if he had a heart attack? What if he's dead in there?*

I knock hard on the back door. "Mr. Sinclair?"

*Maybe he's not dead. Maybe he's dying.*

I pull out my phone to call Mom, then remember the lamp by the barn. Why do I scare myself? He's probably finishing up some chores.

I run into the barn. It's different than ours. The floor is concrete instead of dirt and there aren't any cow stalls. I see a light coming from a room at the back and hear a throbbing hum that sounds like an engine.

"Mr. Sinclair?"

No answer. Maybe he didn't hear me. I go to the room. Mr. Sinclair's not here—but oh my God. On the right are a bunch of refrigeration units. On the left, a table runs along a wall of knives, cleavers, mallets, and saws. Ahead of me, a large, cast-iron laundry tub is filling with chewed-up flesh squeezed out of a large motorized grinder.

I gotta get out of here. I whirl round. Mr. Sinclair's blocking my way.

He steps toward me. "I wondered how long it'd take you to get here."

# 14

M r. Sinclair. I…I…"

"Spit it out."

I back up into the room. "My mother knows I'm here."

"Of course she does. She phoned me last night. Got tired of waiting for you at the house, thought I'd finish grinding some beef." He turns abruptly and walks over to a refrigerator, takes out a square plastic pail, and brings it to the tub. Then he grabs a flat metal scoop from the table and begins to shovel the meat into the pail.

I breathe a little easier. "I didn't see you when I arrived."

"That makes two of us. I was next door in the drying room." I must look pretty clueless because he adds, "It's where I hang the meat."

"Oh. Right."

He snorts. "You one of them kids who think your burger just shows up in the grocery store? Think your eggs grow on trees?"

"No, sir."

"Bet you never seen a grinder like this."

"You're right."

Mr. Sinclair wipes a slick of hair off his forehead with the back of his arm. "It's old, that's for sure. My father bought it back in the fifties. Used to grind things for the fellow who lived over at your place—McTavish. Frank McTavish."

Jacky's father. My heart races. "What sort of things did he grind?"

"Curiosity killed the cat."

I hope he's joking.

Mr. Sinclair scoops the last of the burger meat into the pail. "When I was a boy, food was local, especially in the country. Each farm'd have a few crops, a henhouse, maybe some hogs or dairy. My father butchered the odd cow for the neighbors in exchange for meat. He used the leftovers to make sausages."

He seals the pail and puts it in the fridge. "Mixed farming—gone the way of the dodo. But a few folks still like to know what they're eating. So what the heck? In between planting and harvesting, what else do I have to do but watch the corn grow and worry 'bout the weather?"

Mr. Sinclair glances in my direction. I shrug helpfully like I don't know what else he could be doing either. "Come up to the house," he says. "I pulled out an old photo album with some pictures you might want to see. You were asking about the boy."

"You remembered."

"Why wouldn't I? You think I lost my marbles?"

"No, sir."

"I hope you're right." He shoots me a look. "That was a joke. You can laugh."

"Yes, sir." I smile like I think it was funny.

He shakes his head and we go to the house. It's full of dust, plus that smell that old people get. There's a flypaper strip over the kitchen table that looks like it's been there since last spring.

Mr. Sinclair sits beside me and opens the album. He clicks his tongue as he flips through until he finds the page he's looking for. He taps a picture. "First things first. See anything you recognize?"

"Wow. Our farmhouse in the old days." When it wasn't so run-down. There's a trellis of morning glories on either side of the kitchen window, and the grass has been cut. Three adults sit around a picnic table staring at the camera. I spot Jacky's parents from their wedding picture; neither of them is smiling.

"That's McTavish, in the straw hat, the fellow I told you about," Mr. Sinclair says. "And that's his wife in the polka dots."

I point at the third person in the picture, a chubby woman holding a baby. "Who's that?"

"My mother."

"Is that you she's holding?"

"Well, it isn't the pope."

It's strange seeing grown-ups as babies. I like to imagine them being born with their adult heads, but with Mr. Sinclair that's just *too* weird.

"And your father?" I ask. "Is he the one taking the picture?"

"You're a regular Sherlock Holmes."

I blush. "So your parents were friends of the McTavishes?"

"My father was best man at their wedding, if that's what you're asking. I expect it was on account of they were neighbors and McTavish didn't have anyone else to ask. He was a strange bird. My mother never liked him."

Jacky's parents stare at me from the snapshot. What are they thinking? I flash on Mom and Dad. They had friends who went to their wedding too, friends who came for dinner and took their pictures. Did their friends know about their fights? Did they do or say anything? What about the Sinclairs? Did they know the McTavishes had the kind of problems that made Jacky draw his pictures?

I flash on something else. Cody thinks there was a murder. I thought Jacky got killed, but what if it was his mother? Jacky says she "went away," but what mother runs off without her kid?

"You're pretty quiet all of a sudden," Mr. Sinclair says. "What's on your mind?"

"Nothing. I was just wondering...where's Jacky?"

"Jacky?"

"Wasn't that the name of their son?"

"You do your homework." Mr. Sinclair sits back in his chair. "What else do you know?"

My forehead tingles. What if his family's mixed up in the murder? I thought he agreed to see me to tell me stuff. What if he agreed so he could find out how much I know?

"Not much," I say. "Just his name."

"You sure?"

"Honest."

Mr. Sinclair tilts his head. He doesn't believe me. "Jacky was a year younger than me. He'd have been born a year after this shot was taken."

He flips to a page farther back. The pictures used to be in color, but now they're bleached out. I see a snapshot of two boys playing. They look like ghosts on a pale yellow background. One of them has a Davy Crockett cap. Jacky. Is that the face I saw when I closed my eyes?

I point at the kid, barely able to breathe. "That's him?"

"What makes you say that?"

"The raccoon-skin cap."

"What makes you think Jacky had a raccoon-skin cap?"

"I don't know. Just guessing."

"Well, guess again," Mr. Sinclair says. "*I'm* the one with the cap. When I was really little, every boy wanted to be Crockett, but Frank McTavish didn't have time for things like that. Jacky must've been the only kid without one."

What? If Jacky didn't have a cap, then what I'd imagined was all in my mind. There isn't a ghost after all.

"Happy ending though," Mr. Sinclair continues. "By the time I was twelve or so, the fad was dying out, so I gave my cap to Jacky. He wore it every day. Why, you'd think he'd died and gone to heaven."

"You played with him a lot then?"

"Some. In those days, you didn't have much choice who you played with. It was mostly kids a couple of farms up or down. There wasn't an Internet and only one phone, a landline, for special occasions." He flips through more pages. "See this? Each winter my father made a skating rink in the yard. Jacky and me, we'd pass a puck back and forth. Jacky slid on his boots, no skates. In summer we'd toss a baseball or climb hay in his loft. He was a strange kid. I seem to recall he liked to draw."

"What happened to him?" I ask, all innocent.

"Don't know. His mother ran off, took him with her. Hadn't thought about him much till you asked the other day. Don't have time for memories, too busy making them… That's another joke."

"Sorry." I'm thinking too hard to smile. "What happened to Mr. McTavish?"

"Oh, that was a terrible thing." Mr. Sinclair shakes his head. "Without his wife and boy, McTavish went squirrelier than he already was. Bought a dozen guard dogs. Wild things. My father told me never to go near the place."

He turns the page and taps a picture of the field between his farmhouse and ours. A pack of dogs is running on the bare ground. "Within a few months, those dogs went crazy. Tore him to shreds."

I stare at the dogs. "When did it happen?"

Mr. Sinclair shrugs. "Who knows? Nobody saw it."

"I mean the date." With the date, I can go to the *Weekly Bugle*. I can look up Mr. McTavish's obituary and see if there were suspicions about a murder in the months before he died.

"The date?" Mr. Sinclair shoots me a sly smile. "If I didn't know better, I'd think you were trying to figure out my age. Let's just say early nineteen sixties." He switches the subject to barn raisings, fall fairs, and strawberry socials. He tells me about playing in the hayloft, a girl who fell down an abandoned well, and a man who went to milk his cows in a whiteout and froze to death.

I nod, but I'm hardly listening. All I can think about is Jacky. Jacky, his father, and the dogs.

# 15

I say good night and head back to my place. Good thing I have a flashlight. Mr. Sinclair's corn rises above my head, a forest of darkness. The only sound is my feet on the stones at the side of the road.

Thoughts echo inside my head. *When did Mr. McTavish get killed by the dogs? Where was Jacky? Gone with his mother, or dead and buried?*

A cornstalk snaps in the field. I stop. Whatever I heard stops too. I scan my light across the cornstalks. Is something hiding in there?

*Who cares? It's likely a rabbit or coyote. Either way, they're scared of people.*

I walk faster. There's another crunch from the field. Whatever's out there isn't scared. It's following me. Sounds of panting. Dogs. The dogs. I start to run. So do they. They bound through the stalks beside me.

*No, there's nothing there. It's all in my mind—just my sleeves rubbing against my jacket, my feet on the gravel, my breathing.*

I hear Jacky: "I told you. It's all right. They won't hurt you. I won't let them."

"Leave me alone!"

"But you're my friend."

"Stop! You're freaking me out. Go away!"

I run up the lane to our farm, cornstalks on either side—see the glow of the house lights over the tassels—make the yard—barrel to the door—race inside.

Mom looks up from the sink. "What's the matter? You look as if you've seen a ghost."

"I'm fine." I take off my jacket.

Mom smiles. "Maybe next time you're out at night you'll want a ride."

"No, I won't, and I don't know what you're talking about."

"Cameron, I'm teasing. We both know you have an imagination."

"Right." *Does she have to remind me I'm crazy?*

"So how was your chat with Mr. Sinclair?"

"Okay." I grab a Coke from the fridge and head upstairs.

"Did he have lots to tell you for your essay?" Mom calls after me.

"Uh-huh."

"I can't wait to read it."

*You mean I actually have to write it? Really? Is everyone's mom like this?*

I sit at my desk and look out at the hole in the barn wall where I first thought I saw Jacky. Mr. Sinclair said that before Jacky disappeared, he had a raccoon-skin cap. That fits with what I saw, but lots of kids had caps like that, so maybe it means nothing. He also said Jacky left with his mom. So what's the truth? Did Jacky's father kill him? Or did he just move away?

"Jacky?" I whisper. "Jacky?"

Silence. What did I expect?

I have to talk to Cody. What does he know or *think* he knows? My heart beats faster. How do I talk to Cody without making him mad?

I wake up with the answer. If I can get Cody alone, he won't have to act tough for his gang; and if I tell him I believe in the murder, he won't feel embarrassed. He'll think I'm on his side. Who knows? Maybe he'll start to like me. Or at least stop picking on me.

At lunch, Cody's gang heads to the highway for a smoke. I wait inside the door, sweating. When they start to swagger back, I go out to intercept them. A couple of them bark when they see me coming.

I stick my hands in my pockets so the gang won't see them shake. "Yeah, yeah, the dogs, big deal," I say, like I don't care. "I heard the story. I also heard there's coyotes around. You guys had me going though. And you're right about the house. I want to move—only a freak would wanna live there."

"No kidding," Cody says without smiling. He and his buddies keep walking.

"Hold up."

Cody swings round like he's getting orders from a bug. "Huh?"

I look him in the eye and try not to crap on myself. "Can I talk to you, please?"

Sarcastic "Ooohs" come from the gang.

Cody cocks his head. "What about?"

"It's sort of private."

Cody waves the guys off. They step back. "Okay. What's so private?"

"It's about the murder at my farm," I whisper.

"What murder?" Cody's voice is dead cold.

"You know, the murder back in the sixties. You think there was a murder at my place, right?"

"Who says?"

"I don't know. I just heard."

His fists tighten. "From who? What did they say?"

"Nobody. Nothing."

"They talk about my great-grandma?"

"What? No!"

"Don't lie to me. If they talked about the murder, they talked about her."

"I don't know what you're talking about."

"Liar." Cody shoves me hard on the chest. I go back a few steps. "Who told you? What did they say?"

"Nobody. Nothing. I don't know what you're talking about. I just wanted to say, I think it's true."

"About my great-grandma?"

"No, the murder. I think it happened."

"I'll bet you do." He shoves me again. I fall down. He jumps on top. "Don't ever laugh at my great-grandma. Don't ever talk about my family, you little punk. Got that?"

"I haven't. Not her, your mom, not anybody."

He lifts my shoulders and slams them into the ground. "Why would you talk about Mom?"

"I wouldn't."

"Then why did you say 'your mom'?"

"I didn't mean to. I'm sorry."

"You don't know anything!" He punches me in the face. I hit

back without thinking. He pounds and pounds. A bunch of kids run out to see the show.

"Boys. That's enough." It's Mr. Abbott, a math teacher.

Cody's buddies yank him off me.

"To the office. Both of you. Now."

"Why?" Cody rubs his knuckles. "He started it."

Mr. Abbott takes us to the vice principal. He tells him that Cody did most of the hitting, but he saw me land a punch too.

"What started it?" the VP asks.

"He was talking about my family," Cody says. "Making fun of my great-grandma. Talking about my mom."

"Is that true, Cameron?"

"Not exactly."

Cody glares at me. "I got witnesses."

The VP shoots him a look. "Cody." He looks at me over his glasses. "What do you mean, 'Not exactly'?"

How can I explain without mentioning Benjie, or talking about the murder and sounding nuts? I stare at my hands. "I don't know. I'm not sure. Things didn't come out how I wanted."

There's a zero-tolerance policy for fighting. We both get suspended till the end of the week: three days. The office calls Mom to pick me up.

The drive home takes forever. I try telling Mom it was all a misunderstanding, but she won't listen. "You don't get suspended for nothing." I want to say I was bullied, but it's too embarrassing. If she believed me, she'd think she had to do something, and that would make it worse.

Besides, how do I tell her what got said? Even to me it doesn't make sense. What would Cody's great-grandmother have to do with a murder that no one thinks happened? And why would that make Cody go ballistic?

"A fistfight," Mom says quietly. "That's how it starts."

I feel sick to my stomach. She thinks I'm turning into Dad.

# 16

After supper I go to my room and google Benjie's number. There're only three Dalberts in the area, and the other two are in town. I make the call.

"I told you not to ask Cody about the murder," Benjie says.

"No, you didn't. All you said was, 'Don't tell him there wasn't one.'"

"Oh. Right. I should have been clearer."

"Ya think?"

"Sorry," Benjie says.

"Anyway, I acted like it was true. And now I'm beat up and suspended, and Mom cries when she looks at me. So what's the deal?"

"Well, first thing you should know: Cody's great-grandma is ninety and deranged. A total whack job."

"How do you know?"

"This isn't the city. Everybody knows about everybody. And everybody knows Mrs. Murphy drove her car into the Presbyterian church. Well, not *into* the church, but into the front steps. That's when she lost her license, two years ago. Mom says it was about time—Mrs. Murphy had been parking her car in the middle of the highway and walking off, totally lost."

"No kidding."

"Wait, it gets better. Last year she tried to burn the house down."

"What?"

"Okay, so maybe she didn't *try*. But Cody's grandparents woke up from an afternoon nap and there was a huge fire in the kitchen. His great-grandma had decided to fry something and then wandered out to the barn. There were fire trucks and everything. That's when she got put in the nursing home. She's down the hall from my grandpa. I see her every Sunday and after school on Wednesdays when my folks take me to visit him."

"What's any of this got to do with a murder on my farm?"

"Oh. Yeah. The murder thing." Benjie's so thick they should use his head to stuff pillows. "Okay. So everything I told you about Cody's great-grandma? Kids laughed about it. Cody got into a lot of fights. See, she's the only one in his family who can stand him."

"I get the picture, Benjie. Focus."

"Okay. So anyway, just as Cody's grandparents were getting her into the home, she went mental. Like, swinging-her-cane mental. She screamed they all wanted to lock her up because she knew too much about this murder. Mom told me that, back in the sixties, Mrs. Murphy had accused the man who owned your farm of killing some people."

"You mean the crazy guy who bought the dogs?"

"Right. Only the police investigated and it turned out that nobody killed anybody. It was all in her head. She went quiet for years. Only now she's old and demento, so nothing stops her from saying anything."

"She still talks about the murder?"

"Who knows? I steer clear. I've seen her in the social room sometimes. Her lips move a lot."

My mind whirs: *The police investigated. Nobody killed anybody. Repeat that. Believe it.* But I need to know one last thing. "Benjie, do you remember who she thought the crazy guy murdered?"

"Let's see. His wife and her friend, I think."

"Anyone else?"

"Oh. Yeah," Benjie says. "His son."

# 17

How do I fall asleep after that?

When I finally drift off, it's into a world of nightmares. Jacky's father stuffs people into Mr. Sinclair's grinder. Then he's got a dog's body and chases me through the cornfields. Then I'm hiding in one of the cow stalls as Dad prowls around with a chain saw, shouting, "Hey, Buddy. You can't run from me forever."

"Jacky," I whisper as Dad comes up the aisle, "help me."

"Why? You want me to go away."

"I'm sorry."

"You don't even believe in me. You're mean."

Dad's standing over me. "I got you now, Buddy." He revs the chain saw.

"Jacky! I believe in you! *Help!*"

The alarm goes off. I'm in my room, heart beating so fast it practically bursts out of my chest. I shower, brush my teeth, get dressed, and go downstairs.

Mom's calmer this morning, but I keep my mouth shut all through breakfast. "Be good," she says as she leaves for work.

Normally I'd say, "Always am." Today I settle for, "You bet."

I play Zombie Attack and channel surf, then go back to my room and look at Jacky's drawings. I run my fingers over the pages. Half a century ago, Jacky touched the paper I'm touching. He drew what I'm seeing.

What if Cody's great-grandmother is right? If his father murdered him, did Jacky know it was happening or was it in his sleep? I wonder if Dad ever thought about killing Mom and me. What would he do if he knew Mom was working for C.B.?

*Stop thinking like that.*

I stare out the window at the hole in the barn wall. It'd actually be kind of cool if there *is* a ghost here. At least I'd have someone to talk to. And Jacky, or whatever I've been talking to, has always seemed pretty nice. Weird maybe, but who wouldn't be weird, growing up in the middle of nowhere with a crazy dad and all those dogs? What's wrong with weird anyway? Lots of people think *I'm* weird. Jacky's just lonely. We have a lot in common.

I think for a minute, then whisper, "Jacky? Are you there?" I'm half fooling, but also half hoping, like the time in sixth grade when my buddies and I played with a Ouija board. Part of me was glad nothing spooky happened; the other part was disappointed.

"Jacky?" I whisper again. "Jacky?"

Silence. Oh well, what did I expect? It's not like I believe in ghosts. Even if I did, it's daytime.

"Cameron?" Jacky's voice is coming from the doorway. "You sure you want me here? Because I can go away. I don't want to scare you. I just want a friend."

I try to act normal. "I'm fine, Jacky. Really. I'm glad you're here. I'm sorry for what I said."

Jacky smiles. "Good."

I turn around slowly. There's nothing in the doorway, but when I close my eyes I see him, all shy and awkward. It seems totally real, like something in a dream, only I'm wide awake. It's the weirdest, most amazing thing that's happened to me since, like, forever.

"So, do you want to do something?" Jacky asks.

"Like what?"

"I don't know. Go play in the barn? It's fun out there."

"Sure."

"Come on then."

I open my eyes and hear Jacky calling me from the kitchen. "What's keeping you?" I go downstairs, put on my jacket, and step outside.

I picture Jacky skipping into the barn. I follow him inside. I imagine him in the shadows, sitting on the side of a cow stall.

"I gave the cows names," Jacky says. "Pepper was in here. She was white with black splotches. Salt was black with white ones. Other cows I named after characters in my comic books. Every fall, Father brought some of them over to Arty's, and his father butchered them for us to eat or sell in town. I cried when he took Pepper, but he slapped the back of my head and told me not to be a baby. Mother said I shouldn't think of them as pets."

"That's rough. Did you ever have a real pet?"

"Not really." Jacky sighs. "We had barn cats, but I couldn't bring them into the house. Anyway, if you went to pet them, they'd hiss and run away. That's why I liked the cows. They let you stroke their sides. You couldn't ride them though. I tried to climb onto Pepper once, but she didn't like it. I nearly got stomped."

"What about the dogs?"

"Are you kidding?" Jacky looks around as if somebody might be listening. "I was scared of the dogs. They did things. Awful things."

"Like?"

"Like with the rabbits. I saw out my window." Jacky's eyes widen in terror. He sticks his fingers in his ears and sings, *"La-la-la-la-la-la!"* like I used to do when Mom and Dad fought.

"Jacky! It's not happening now!"

But he's gone; I'm talking to the air. I'm about to go back to the house when I hear him in the hayloft. I go up the stairs. When I enter the loft, birds fly down from the rafters. I look up and picture Jacky swinging his legs from a crossbeam.

"This is my favorite place," he says like everything's fine. "Before the dogs, me and Arty played here all the time. The hay was all piled. We'd climb it and slide down. It made us real itchy, but that didn't stop us."

"Sounds like you and Mr. Sinclair—Arty—were good friends."

"Best friends. He gave me this cap." Jacky strokes the raccoon tail.

"That was just before you left with your mom, right?"

"Huh? Who says I left with Mother?"

"Arty."

Jacky shakes his head. "Mother left without me. Arty knows that."

"How does he know?"

"It's a secret."

"Why?"

"Because." He vanishes.

"Jacky?"

"Over here."

I turn and see him crouching by the hole in the barn wall.

"Father used to pile all the cow pies under here," Jacky says. "In the summer the sun dried the outside of them all crusty so they didn't smell. One day, when we were little, Arty and I got tired of sliding down the hay. We crawled through the opening here and slid down the cow pies instead. Arty's folks thought it was funny, but Father gave me the belt."

"The belt?"

"You know, when your father takes his belt and whips you."

"Your father whipped you?"

"Only when I deserved it. He didn't want to. It was just so I'd be good. 'This hurts me more than it does you.' That's what he'd tell Mother and me when we were bad. If Mother had been good, she wouldn't have run away. Then Father wouldn't have gotten the dogs and everything would be okay." Jacky shudders.

"Are you all right?"

"I can't talk now. I hear things. I see things." He disappears into the air for good, but his words keep repeating: "I hear things. I see things." Only he's not the one talking; I am.

I stop and the barn goes so quiet I'm afraid to breathe. It's like I'm in another world: now and *not* now, all at once.

*What did Jacky see? What did he hear?*

My eyes see double, triple. As things blur, I picture hay sloping up to the back rafters. I imagine the squishy feel of it and the smell.

The smell of the cows too—a damp, funky smell—and the sound of them shuffling and snorting in their stalls below. Jacky and Arty scramble up the heap, the hay giving way under their feet. They roll down, laughing.

One blink and my vision clears. Cool. Next I crouch where Jacky crouched and look at the house. I imagine it from Mr. Sinclair's photographs, with fresh paint and a band of petunias on either side of the back shed door. The McTavishes' car is in the drive, a fifties Chevy, green with fins.

In my head I hear a radio playing and Jacky's mother singing along. All of a sudden there's a man's voice and a fight. Jacky's mom screams, "You want to hit me? Hit me where the bruise will show, coward."

Wait. That's Mom's voice. My heart skips and I'm back in the here and now. *Did Mom ever say that? Did I ever hear it?*

I need some air.

# 18

Mom's back at five. She calls me to the kitchen table. I sit like a prisoner waiting to be executed. Will it be the "I'm disappointed" speech or the "I love you" speech? I know she loves me. I know she's disappointed. Why does she have to say it?

Mom reaches across the table and puts her hand on mine. "Cameron," she says softly, "I want to apologize."

What? I stare down at our hands. Mom still wears her wedding ring. She says it's to keep men away, but it reminds me of Dad. I wonder if it reminds her.

"I should never have said what I said yesterday about a fight being the beginning," Mom says. "You are not your father. You are you. And who you are is a good, kind, bright young man who cares about people."

My insides quiver. *I'm not good. I'm not kind. I think mean thoughts about people. I go behind your back. I lie. I make things up. I'm a horrible person. I'm...*

"Cameron?"

I wipe the corner of my eye. "It's okay."

Mom hands me a Kleenex. Somehow she always has a

Kleenex. "I want you to know that what's been happening with you these past few weeks, what you've been going through, isn't your fault."

*Is this about me being picked on at school? Eating lunch alone in a bathroom stall? Did I say Jacky's name in my sleep?*

"I don't know exactly what's going on in your head"—what a relief—"but I see the signs. The nightmares. The talking to yourself."

I want to crawl in a hole.

"It's all right, Cameron. I understand." *You don't.* "It's been like this ever since you were a child. Whenever you have a problem, you go off into your own world. I can be talking to you, others can, but it's like you don't hear us. Since this last move it's gotten worse."

I'm afraid to ask, but I have to. "What about my lips?"

Mom squeezes my hand. "I know you try hard to keep them from moving. And when that doesn't work, you try to cover your mouth. You're so good about that. But yes, they've been moving. Not always, but sometimes."

"Am I loud?"

"No, no. Very quiet, sometimes no sound at all."

*Am I like that at school? Who else has seen me?*

"I don't know who you're talking to, but it can be pretty intense."

"Myself. I'm just talking to myself. Lots of people do."

"I know. But lately…lately I watch you, and you don't even notice me watching. It's a worry."

"Why?" As if I don't know the answer.

"Because it's not normal, Cameron. It's not just the talking to yourself either. You frown all the time. You don't communicate. Sometimes you hit yourself."

"When?"

"Different times. Not often. It doesn't matter."

"It matters to me. If I was hitting myself, I think I'd know about it."

"I'd hope so," Mom says carefully. "And then there are the nightmares. You wake up drenched in sweat, and even though you know I'm there, it's like you're in another world."

I swallow hard. "You think I'm crazy."

"No. But I think you have problems. You're troubled."

I go to say something, but there's nothing to say.

"Cameron, it's nothing to be ashamed of. You've gone through such terrible things. But you're not alone. I want to help."

*You can't.*

"Please let me."

*How?*

Mom takes a breath. "I was talking to Ken."

Cowboy Boots? "You talked about me to *him*?"

"I didn't say much."

"He's a jerk. A phony."

"Cameron, he's a nice man who's given me work—work that puts a roof over our heads and food on the table."

"That gives him a right to hear about my private life?"

"No. All I said is, you're at an age when you might want a man to talk to. Most boys have a father."

My stomach churns. "So do I. Only you won't let me see him."

"That isn't fair."

"What, that I have a father I can't see? No, it *isn't* fair." I pull my hand away.

Mom tries not to look upset. "You don't have to talk to Ken if you don't want to, but he'd be happy to talk to you."

I look her in the eye. "Are you going out with him?"

"What?"

"Is this your way of introducing 'the kid'?"

"Cameron, that's out of line."

"So I'm right."

"No. You're *wrong*."

"Because no way will that jerk ever be my father. I have a father. And if I ever need to talk to a man who *isn't* my father, I'll talk to Mr. Sinclair."

"Fine."

"So can I go now?"

"You can go."

I push my chair back, get up, and head up the stairs.

"Cameron," she calls after me, "I love you."

"Right." I don't turn back. No way she's going to see me cry.

# 19

All night I worry about Mom thinking I'm crazy. She thinks Dad's crazy too. Is she right? Are we both nuts? I also stress about Jacky. Mr. Sinclair says he left with his mom. Jacky says he didn't, that Mr. Sinclair saw him after she was gone. Who's telling the truth? Why would either of them lie?

*How can anyone know anything about anyone? How can anyone be sure even about themselves?*

Only one thing's certain: Jacky's a secret I can't tell anybody.

Mom's gone by the time I get up. I make myself toast and jam, take a tub of ice cream to the kitchen window, and look out at the woods behind the corn. The sun is bright, the sky is clear—what a perfect day to explore. If I hadn't been suspended, I'd be on the bus right now, taunted by Cody's gang, smelling Benjie's breath, and worried about today's science test. I should get suspended more often.

I bundle up and head out to the field. My view of the woods is blocked by the corn—it's way taller than I am—but if I walk straight forward I can't help but bump into it. After the first few rows it gets hard to see anything, what with the leaves. It's tougher to move than I figured too. The worst part is the cobs hitting my face and the tassels going up my nose. On the plus side, there's the smell of the corn, so sweet and fresh I can taste it.

I wade forward, but it takes, like, forever. It's got to be fifteen minutes since I started. Shouldn't I at least be seeing the treetops over the stalks? Maybe I should head back.

*No, that's dumb. For all I know, I'm almost there. Besides, quitting's for losers.*

I keep going. Still no sign of the woods. Am I heading in the right direction? Have I gotten turned around?

An engine revs over at Mr. Sinclair's. I'm so busy keeping tassels out of my eyes that it takes me a while to realize the sound is getting louder. Make that closer. Why would an engine be getting closer?

*Oh my God, it's not any old engine. It's Mr. Sinclair's combine. He's harvesting the field. And I'm in the middle of it.*

I picture blades slicing through stalks—and *me*! I have to get out of here. But where to? Where am I? Which way do I go?

*Don't panic. Figure out where Mr. Sinclair's headed and go someplace else.*

How? I can't see him. The corn's too high.

*So? If he gets close, jump out of the way.*

Jump? I can hardly walk.

*Then yell. He'll hear you.*

Over the noise?

I try to run. The more I try, the more the corn gets in my way. I force the stalks aside with both arms like I'm doing the breaststroke. It doesn't matter. I'm not getting anywhere. I gasp for breath. Leaves and tassels hit my face, get in my nose and mouth. I'm flailing, drowning. "Help!"

*It's all right.*

Jacky? Is that you?

*Breathe.*

The engine's deafening.

"Mr. Sinclair! Stop!" I wave my arms.

*He can't see or hear you. Breathe.*

"I can't."

*You can. You're almost at the woods. Look ahead to the right.*

Out of nowhere, I spot a trail between the corn rows. Why didn't I see it before? I can't hear myself think—just the voice in my head yelling, *Now! Run!*

I push through to the trail. See treetops over the stalks. Break through them and race from the field, out of danger. I did it. I'm at the woods.

I drop to my knees. "Jacky, you saved my life." He doesn't say anything. "Jacky?" He's gone.

I catch my breath. I can't believe I'm alive. I get up and brush myself off. Guess I'm stuck here till Mr. Sinclair takes a break.

I look up and down the tree line. The woods run across the back of five farms, but I don't know how deep they go. I should stay near the edge so I don't get lost. Last thing I need is Mom calling a search party while I'm suspended.

Still, it can't be a forest or anything. I mean there are farms all around, and Jacky and Mr. Sinclair played here. Besides, past the bushes, the trees are fairly spaced out. Some look good for climbing.

That could be fun—scrambling up to the top to look back at the house or to spy on Mr. Sinclair harvesting. I think of Jacky's drawings of the two of them in the treetops. I wonder what they saw.

Before I climb any trees though, I want to check out the clearing. It's not far—a big swath of sunlight. Dead branches lie scattered along the way, like deer antlers. There are a few fallen trees too, rotten and covered in moss. One's really long with big roots pointing up to the sky.

When Jacky made his drawings, a lot of these trees wouldn't have been around. The fallen ones would've been healthy, and the ones that were rotting then are long gone now, with nothing to show they existed. Trees are like people. We're alive, then we're memories, then we're not even that.

Mom says that kind of talk is morbid, but it's true. I have no idea what my great-grandparents looked or sounded like, or the great-greats before them, back to caveman days. It's weird to think they were like me once, goofing with friends, mad at their parents, brave, scared, everything. But now they're gone and all the people and things that mattered to them are gone too, and nobody knows or cares. So why do I make myself miserable over things that years from now no one will even care about? If I knew that, maybe I could be happy.

When I hit the clearing, the gloom disappears in a blaze of sunshine. The leaves are turning orange and red, and there are patches of berry bushes. There's an outcrop of rock too, and in the center—my heart skips—the boulders from Jacky's pictures.

I imagine Jacky and Mr. Sinclair pretending the boulders are their fort. Then I see Jacky, alone, hiding in the treetops, pretending his father doesn't exist.

A bird chirps. I stand still, hoping to glimpse it. Everything's quiet. How come I don't hear the combine? I get a creepy feeling someone's watching me. I glance over my shoulder.

Mr. Sinclair's at the edge of the clearing. "What are you doing crossing a field mid-harvest? You want to get yourself killed?"

"Sorry. I was already halfway before you started. How did you know I was here?"

"I saw the stalks move. Good thing too. I figured it was you; came to bring you home. Don't want your mother getting back and me having to explain how come you're mashed up in my corn cobs." He snorts. "Or maybe I could just grind you up and have her think you ran away."

I laugh like this is a joke, but he just stares at me. I think about Jacky and his mother disappearing. I stop laughing.

"Why aren't you in school anyway?" Mr. Sinclair says.

"I got suspended. It wasn't my fault."

"If I had a dollar for every time something wasn't someone's fault…" Mr. Sinclair's voice trails off. "So you thought you'd check out the woods. What did you think you'd find?"

"Nothing. I just wanted to see where you and Jacky played."

"Who says we played here?"

"I guessed."

"So you're a guesser, are you? What kind of guesser? A guesser who guesses he knows, or a guesser who knows he guesses?"

"I guess I don't know."

Mr. Sinclair cracks a smile. "You're not as stupid as you look." He nods at the boulders. "I used to leave things there for Jacky to find. A magnifying glass. A bag of marbles. Things I didn't want anymore. I told him elves left them. He knew it was me, but it was more fun to pretend." Mr. Sinclair's eyes soften.

"Do you ever wonder what happened to him?"

His eyes narrow. "Why would I?"

"I don't know; you were friends. I think about *my* friends, the ones I've left behind. I hope they think about me."

"I wouldn't count on it. Nobody thinks about anybody these days. By the time you're my age, you can't even remember how many friends have disappeared."

"Like Jacky?"

Mr. Sinclair grunts. "He was like you. Disappeared with his mother."

*Not according to Jacky.*

"What are you thinking?"

"Nothing," I say.

"Nobody thinks nothing."

"Okay… I was just wondering if Jacky ever talked about his father."

"Why would he do that? Do you talk about yours?"

"That's different."

"Is it?" Mr. Sinclair watches me squirm. "You're not the only guesser around here. Everybody has secrets. It's best to leave them alone. Come along now. I'll drive you back to the house. I have work to do."

## 20

Everyone has secrets, like Mr. Sinclair said. Mom, Dad, me. What are Mr. Sinclair's secrets? And Jacky's? Back at the house I ask Jacky, "Why didn't your mother take you with her like Mom took me?"

I know he's listening. I can feel him all around, peeking at me from behind furniture, hiding in closets, under the bed, but he won't come out. Is he playing a game? What's his story?

I take out his drawings and look for clues I might have missed the first time. There's a black shape in some of the drawings. Is it a hole or a cave or the coal room? Maybe it's just a scribble. And what about the picture of his mother on the ground? Is she sleeping? Dead? There are things in the drawings that could give me nightmares too—ordinary things like his father's shovel, ax, and pitchfork.

As I stare at the pictures, the room disappears. I feel the present in the past, the past in the present. Jacky walked on these floorboards, touched these doorknobs and handrails like I do. He used the same sink, bathtub, and desk. Jacky's everywhere. He's in the air I breathe.

I imagine him moving around up here and find myself in the

big room over the kitchen, staring up at the trapdoor to the attic. *Why is it sealed shut?* I could chisel away the caked paint and claw out the nails, but I'd make a mess. Mom would freak. *What's in the attic, Jacky? What's its secret?*

"Cameron?" Mom's voice is coming from the kitchen.

"I'm upstairs," I call down in a super cheery voice. *How long has Mom been home? Did she hear me talking to myself?*

"I've got us pizza," Mom calls back, in a super cheery voice of her own. "Double cheese, pepperoni, and mushroom. It just needs a minute in the microwave."

If Mom heard me, she's pretending she didn't. Good. Let's pretend together.

"Great. Thanks. I'll be right down."

Mom smiles as I sit down at the table. "How was your day?" You'd never guess we had a fight last night. Mom doesn't forget fights, but she's good at packing them away. They're like Christmas decorations—hidden from view but easily pulled from storage.

"My day? Pretty good." I pick up a slice of pizza. "I did a lot of homework."

"Good." Mom pauses. "Would you like to come into town with me tomorrow?"

"Huh?"

"After two days here alone, you must be getting a bit stir-crazy."

"What would I do?"

"There's a library, a recreation center. Or don't come. Stay here and be bored. It's up to you."

"No, it could be good." It could be too.

The rest of dinner is okay. We stick to safe topics, like where we'll meet up for lunch. Luckily the high school's on the country side of the bridge, so it's not like any of the guys will see us.

"By the way, I didn't forget about your project," Mom says when we finish eating. She brings me a thick package from the counter. "The sales history of the farm."

"Thanks."

"Ken's the one you should thank. He says if you need anything else, just ask."

I give her a look. "Didn't we talk about me and *Ken*?"

"I told him about your project *before* our conversation. He said he was going to the registry office today and could check about the farm while he was there."

"Fine. Just so I don't owe him anything."

"You don't, except a thank-you."

"I don't want *you* to owe him anything either."

"Cameron." Mom sighs. "Sometimes people do favors without wanting anything. It's called being nice."

Mom's pretty smart, but she sure doesn't know guys.

I take the package upstairs, sit cross-legged on my bed, and empty it. There's tons of stuff. No way this is a "no big deal" favor. This is a "Hey, Katherine, see what a great guy I am, getting all this stuff for your son? How about dinner?" favor.

There's a note from C.B. on company stationery that has his picture at the top. I take a pen, black out a couple of teeth, and give him a unibrow.

*Hey Cameron,*

*Heard about your history project. Glad to help.*

*I asked Arlene Cooper at the registry office to print out some survey maps, the sales history, and the yearly tax statements. Most farms around here are passed down to sons, so the tax statements are actually more useful than the sales history for knowing who owned the place.*

*Your mother says you're especially interested if there was ever a murder or suicide on your farm. Wish I could say yes to juice up your essay, but nothing came up. There was once a farmer who was killed by his dogs though. Maybe that's just as good?*

*Let me know if you have any other questions. Also, let me know if you'd like to toss a baseball, shoot some hoops.*

*Ken*

*Toss a baseball? Shoot some hoops? Gag me.*

The most important thing is, C.B. says there wasn't a murder. So what happened to Jacky? If he didn't leave with his mom, wouldn't he have been found after the dogs killed his father?

I look at the maps. Interesting. The one of the county in 1825 shows the rail line that used to run through Wolf Hollow. The 1838 township survey has half the area as woods.

The sheaf of tax assessments underneath is an inch thick. I

almost fall asleep just looking at it. I toss it aside and glance at the one-page summary of the farm's sales history.

Weird. The first owner, Silas Henning, bought the farm in 1839. It stayed in his family till 1924, when it was sold to Henry McTavish. And that's it. The farm was never sold again. *That can't be right. What about the sale to the Sinclairs?*

I grab the tax assessments. The name Henry McTavish changes to Frank McTavish in 1952. That would be when Jacky's father took over. Mr. McTavish's name is on the assessments up to this year.

That means Mr. Sinclair doesn't own the farm. It's still owned by Jacky's father. A dead man. What's Mr. Sinclair hiding—about the farm, about Jacky, about everything?

# 21

I show Mom that Mr. McTavish still owns the farm.

"My, that's curious, isn't it?" She tries not to smile. "I'm not a real estate agent, so I'm afraid I don't have an answer to the mystery, but I know someone who *is* a real estate agent, and I'm sure he'd love to clear it up for you."

*Nice one, Mom.*

But she's right. C.B. *is* the one I need to talk to. Damn.

Next morning, the sun has a harder time getting up than I do. As we drive to town, fog drifts across the harvested fields.

We slow down as we near the school; a couple of buses are turning into the parking lot. I slide low in my seat so no one will see me. A few seconds later, we're driving past the motel where we stayed our first night and over the old iron bridge into town.

I look down at the river ravine running under the bridge—the hollow in Wolf Hollow. The heaviest part of the fog is settling in the gully. It's like we're driving over clouds. I imagine the old days, with wolves coming up through the mist.

After the bridge, the highway turns into the main drag, a.k.a. Main Street. There's only maybe ten streets that cut across and seven or eight that run parallel on either side. We pass a soft ice-cream drive-through that's closed till spring, a tiny strip mall with a burger joint, 7-Eleven, a gas station, and the post office. After that, a bunch of two-story buildings, with stores and restaurants on the main floor and people living above: the Knotty Pine Inn; Mindy's Fine Dining; Walker's Ladies' and Men's Apparel, with clothes for people who apparently lived a century ago; the Shamrock Bar, with shuttered windows; Lucille's Nail Emporium; Lucky Laundromat; two drugstores; and Wolf Hollow's one and only movie theater, the Capital, which only has two screens.

In the middle of Main Street, things get respectable again with the town hall, the registry office, the police station, the library, and the *Weekly Bugle* offices. Then there's a house covered in shingles with painted wooden butterflies nailed on the walls and a homemade sign that says Kelly's Krafts; Huntley Memorials with a front yard covered in tombstones; and another small strip mall, home to a dollar store, Minnie's Mini-Mart, and Ken Armstrong Realty. Finally, a gas station for anyone who forgot to fill up at the other end of town, and then back to farms.

We pull up in front of the agency at eight thirty. C.B. hasn't arrived.

"Not to worry, he'll be here any minute," Mom says. "Then you can solve your mystery, have your swim at the rec center, and meet me here at noon for lunch. The Knotty Pine Inn has great fries. And homemade fruit pies. You'll love it."

I sling my backpack over my shoulder and follow Mom inside, where I leave C.B.'s package on her desk. Then I go back out and pass the time looking at the pictures of homes for sale in the front window, all of them better than our place.

I hear an electric drill at Huntley Memorials. Through the fog I see a stumpy, middle-aged man in overalls, work boots, goggles, and a baseball cap engraving a granite stone resting on a picnic table. A long, orange extension cord runs from his chisel into a cinder-block garage.

I walk over for a look-see. The guy has the roughest hands I've ever seen. Scraggy hair sticks out from under his cap and runs down the back of his neck. He turns off his chisel and looks up. "Can I help you?"

"Not really. I'm just waiting for Mr. Armstrong. Uh, Ken Armstrong Realty? My mom works for him. I saw you working and, well, I've never seen anybody carving a gravestone."

"Oh."

The way he says it, I'm not sure if I'm supposed to leave or say something else. I nod at the stone. "Did that guy just die?"

"Month ago."

"Oh." Awkward pause. "Was he a friend?" *Did I just say that? What's wrong with me?*

"No. Why?"

"No reason." *Leave. Leave now.* "So, like, what happens if you spell a name wrong?"

"I don't. Anything else?"

Suddenly I have a brainstorm. Mr. McTavish got his dogs right after his wife disappeared; they killed him a few months after. If I know when he died, I can figure the in-between time when Cody's great-grandmother accused him of murder and check what she said at the *Bugle*.

I clear my throat. "Does your family do all the gravestones around here?"

"Pretty much." He tosses his chin at his sign: Huntley Memorials. Established 1926.

"So your family would've done the stone for Frank McTavish?"

The man pauses. "Who?"

"He was the farmer who got ripped apart by his dogs, sometime in the sixties."

"Oh, that guy."

"Yeah. I need the date he died. It'd be on his stone, right?"

"Sure, but you're talking fifty years ago. We don't keep records back that far. And we sure don't keep track of inscriptions."

*Why not? What's the matter with you?*

The guy leans over the stone and gets back to work. "If you really want to know, try the cemetery. Two blocks over, turn right, end of the road, just before the lake. They'll have a map of who's buried where. Check his grave."

The cemetery. I'm on my way.

# 22

Before I can take off, C.B. wheels up in his car and leaps out like the buddy sidekick on some cop show. "Cameron, my man, what's up?" He raises his hand like he actually expects me to high-five him.

I give him a half-assed wave and put my hands in my pockets. "It's about the package you sent me, the stuff about the farm. There's something weird. Mom said you might be able to explain it."

"Sure thing." He waves me into the agency.

Mom's on the phone. She gives me a *Be good* look and mouths, "Coffee, please," to C.B. He winks a *You betcha*, and pushes a button on the coffee machine.

"You want a cappuccino?" he asks me.

"Sure."

Mom raises an eyebrow. She knows I hate coffee. I shoot her a *Don't embarrass me* look.

C.B. hands Mom the first one, and they banter till ours are ready. I put four packs of sugar in mine, retrieve the package from Mom's desk, and follow C.B. to his private office. It's a beige room with sheer curtains that cover a barred window facing the rear alley. The walls are covered in frames: his college degree, his real estate license, cheesy slogans like "If Not Now, When?" and pictures of a girl and boy around four or five. I stop at the one where the kids are squeezed together on the top step of a porch eating ice-cream cones.

C.B. comes over. "Patrick and Kimberley."

"Your kids?"

"They're seven and eight now," he says, nodding. "Live with their mother a few hundred miles away. I don't get to see them so much."

"You're divorced?"

"Pretty much. There's still some paperwork. But yeah." For a second he doesn't sound like a TV ad; he's like a guy who just misses his kids.

C.B. sits in the leather chair behind his desk and motions me to the one opposite. He breathes in his cappuccino. I take a sip and try not to make a face.

"I can't wait to hear your questions. Your mom says you're always thinking. A real brain. I gotta tell you, I'm not. But you're smart enough to already know that, right?" Is he trying to get me to like him? Is he saying he knows I don't?

"I'm not so bright."

"Don't kid a kidder," he says, laughing. "Luckily I'm good at real estate. Luckier still, I like it. Anyway, something I sent you needs explaining?"

"Yeah." I hand him the package. "According to the sales page, the Sinclairs never bought the farm, and taxes are still made out to Frank McTavish, the guy who was killed by the dogs."

"What?"

"You didn't know?"

"No." C.B. frowns, pulls out the material, and scans it. "I told Arlene what I wanted. She did the printouts and I passed them straight on." He checks back and forth between the pages. "Wow."

"'Wow' is right. I mean, how is this even possible?"

"Good question." C.B. leans back in his chair. He told me to ask him anything, but he's stumped by my first question. I watch the pressure build on his forehead. It's almost enough to make me feel sorry for him.

"Okay," he says at last, "but this is only a guess. If I recall the story, McTavish's wife left with their son a short time before he died. His will would likely have named his son to inherit the farm."

"But if the son was missing…"

"…and McTavish had no other family to claim it, the farm would have sat there. Unpaid taxes would have piled up and the county would've taken it to settle the debts."

"Unless somebody *paid* the taxes," I say, "in which case the county would be happy?"

"Sure. Nobody'd want to step in if there was a son who might come back someday."

"So if Mr. Sinclair's family paid the taxes, they'd be able to use the land for free until the son returned."

"Your mom's right. You're smart."

"But the son, Jacky, *never* came back," I exclaim, the thoughts coming as fast as I can say them. "Nobody cared though, because the taxes were being paid, and eventually so much time passed that nobody thought about it anymore. It was just the way things were."

"Sure is a possibility."

"Is that legal?"

"Well, it's not *il*legal. Especially if McTavish had named Art Sinclair's father as his executor—the guy taking care of his will."

"Mr. Sinclair said his dad and Mr. McTavish were best friends."

"There you are, then." C.B. drums his fingers on his desk. "Art's father could easily have said he was looking after the farm till McTavish's son was found. And there'd be nothing and no one to make him sell it."

"And then Mr. Sinclair's father dies, and Mr. Sinclair just keeps paying the taxes like his family's done since forever, and he gets to make money off a farm he never paid for."

C.B.'s eyes flicker. He knows where I'm headed, and where I'm headed is trouble. "Remember, that's just a guess, Cameron. Even if we're right, at this point Mr. Sinclair could likely claim squatter's rights. If I were him, I'd go to court and make it official."

"But there's a chance he could lose. So maybe he thinks, why risk it?"

C.B. laughs. "More likely, knowing Art, he's just never gotten around to it. Personally, I'd have it at the top of my to-do list. I hate uncertainty."

"Me too."

We share a look.

"What?" he asks with a smile.

"What do you mean, what?"

"You want to ask me something."

"How do you know?"

"The way you're sitting."

"You're a pretty good guesser."

"Sales." C.B. taps his temple.

"Okay." I hesitate. "If this is too personal just say so, but…what's it like not seeing your kids so much?"

He looks me straight in the eye. "It's a bit like dying. They're my kids. But they'll never live with me again. And they're doing things I'm not part of. Creating memories I'll never share. It kills me. Yeah. It kills me."

*Does Dad miss me like that? Is that why he still tries to find me?*

"How often do you see them?"

"One weekend a month. A week at Christmas. Two weeks in the summer. It's not like you and your dad."

I freeze. "How much did Mom tell you?" It comes out sounding mad, but that's not how I mean it. I don't know *how* I mean it. All Mom did was talk to a friend. And it's not like he's as bad as I thought.

"Cameron," he says, like his eyes are seeing into my brain, like his voice is giving me a hug, "whatever is between you and your mom and your dad—that's between the three of you. It's none of my business."

"Right." I can feel my face doing everything not to crumple up.

"Another thing: I know you already have a dad, and he's not me, and I'll never be him. I'll never try to be either. I promise. I'll only ever be me. Ken. Talk to me, don't talk to me, it's up to you. Just know I'm here."

"Okay."

We both seem to know the conversation is over. It's weird how that happens. We go see Mom at the front.

"Did you work out the ownership question?" Mom asks.

"We worked out a lot of things," Ken says.

Mom turns to me. "So, it's nine o'clock. You'll be back here at noon after your swim?"

"Sure." If there's a swimming pool at the cemetery. "See you." I swing my backpack over my shoulder and head out the door with them calling, "Have fun," after me.

I don't look back. I don't want to know if he puts his hand on her shoulder. For now, all I know is that I'm not going to call him C.B. anymore. From now on, he's Ken.

# 23

The cemetery. It's all I can think about.

I go two blocks over and turn right, like the man from Huntley's said, and walk down a street of old brick homes. They all have verandas with bushes at the side, big windows, and a tree near the sidewalk. A few have a cement birdbath. After the fourth street, the houses get shabbier. Some houses have dented aluminum siding. Crabgrass is growing through cracks in the cement sidewalks, and one place has a rusty jungle gym. Then I'm passing a small park.

The farther I go, the foggier it gets. It's like moving through sheets of cobwebs. Finally I come to the final crossroad. On the other side are a spiked wrought-iron fence and a wooden sign by an open gate that says: Wolf Hollow Cemetery, est. 1794.

I follow the road through the gate into a world of tombstones. How will I ever find Mr. McTavish? The road divides in two. The right fork leads to a small building with a garage and toolshed. There's a light in the window. I knock on the door.

"Ya-llow," comes a voice from inside. The door opens. I'm staring at a short, stocky woman in a bright yellow raincoat and work gloves. "What can I do you for?"

"I'm looking for a grave."

"Then you've come to the right place." She winks. "Any grave in particular?"

"Yes. Frank McTavish. He died a long time ago."

"You're asking me?"

*Seriously, what is it with people around here?*

The woman waves me into a bare-bones office lit by a panel of fluorescents. There's a wall heater, a desk with a computer, and the kind of chairs you see at garage sales. On the walls are bleached-out pictures of gardens and rainbows, and a large survey map of the cemetery grounds.

"Jean Currie." She shakes my hand.

"Cameron Weaver."

"And you're looking for Frank McTavish. He's the one got ripped apart by his dogs, right? I don't need the computer for him. Those dogs, they're a bit of a local legend." She taps the cemetery map. "He's planted with his parents in Section D, Plot 24. You take the main road up to the second turnoff. After a while you'll come to a big maple tree on your right. Walk a bit on an eighty-degree angle, and there you go."

I feel like a lost puppy. I must look like one too.

"All righty, I'll take you myself," Ms. Currie sighs, like I'm her good deed of the day. "Have to dig a hole in Section F anyhow. Gentleman from the nursing home, died the day before yesterday, ninety-six. They say he had a good dinner, then bingo. Hard to complain."

*Rewind.* "You dig graves?"

"Groundskeeper, grave digger, that's me."

Ms. Currie brings me to the garage and has me sit beside her on the backhoe loader. We drive through the fog.

"You should come when it's sunny," Ms. Currie says. "Beautiful. In the summer, tourists drop by to do rubbings of the pioneer stones."

When we get to the maple, Ms. Currie parks the backhoe and walks me over to Mr. McTavish's grave. The marker is a plain gray slab of limestone.

McTAVISH

EMILY (COLE) McTAVISH

MARCH 12, 1899–APRIL 24, 1924

BELOVED WIFE OF

HENRY K. McTAVISH

JAN. 18, 1893–FEBRUARY 16, 1952

PARENTS OF

FRANK H. McTAVISH

APRIL 24, 1924–JUNE 1964

Strange. All the dates have a day, except for Jacky's father. If they only knew the month he died, not the day, he could've been dead for weeks before they found him. I imagine his body in the field with stuff growing up around it. I imagine the Sinclairs knocking at his door, wondering where he is. I imagine them figuring he's off somewhere and leaving, and him only a few hundred yards away, half eaten by his dogs. By the time they found him, how much was left?

"Are you okay?" Ms. Currie asks.

"Sure, yeah." *Not.* "I just noticed something. Mr. McTavish's mother died the day he was born."

Ms. Currie peers at the dates. "Say, you're pretty observant. Must have been childbirth. Happened a lot back then."

"And there's no second wife named, so it looks like his father never remarried. He had no other family?"

"Not that I can tell. This plot has room for six and there's just the three of them." Ms. Currie pauses. "Don't mean to rush, kiddo, but I have to get digging. You can find your way back?"

"Yes, thanks. I just take the turnoff back to the road."

"That's the ticket." She heads back to her backhoe. "See you later, alligator."

"In a while, crocodile." I haven't said that since I was five or six with Grandma.

Ms. Currie drives off into the fog. I kneel in front of the gravestone and read and reread the inscription for Jacky's father. He was born in 1924 and died in 1964. That means he was forty. Dad's age. This could be Dad's grave.

I put my hand on the cold stone and close my eyes. I see the picture Dad gave me at our last visit, the one of him and me at the beach, the one I keep hidden behind the picture of Mom and my grandparents on my bedside table. Does Dad still look like he did then? Does he wonder what *I* look like? What if he dies and I never see him again?

Something's behind me. I turn my head. Through the mist I see a large, gray dog staring at me from beside a tombstone.

*What does it want?*

Don't think crazy. It's just a dog. An ordinary dog.

*Is it?*

The dog's eyes are ice blue. I press my back against Mr. McTavish's gravestone. The dog disappears in the mist. I stay frozen against the stone for what seems like forever. All I see are gravestones, angels, and crosses. I get up slowly and head toward the maple tree at the side of the turnoff.

*Something's following me. Something's behind the stones.*

I follow the turnoff to the main road. Suddenly, there it is again, right ahead of me, blocking my way: the dog.

"Go away. Leave me alone."

The dog growls. There's no one to help me. I think of Mr. McTavish. Then I hear a faraway voice: "Don't be afraid. He won't hurt you. I won't let him."

The dog runs off.

"Jacky?" I whisper. "Are you here?"

"No. At the farm. I haven't left the farm since Mother went away. I told you that."

I close my eyes. I expect to picture him in the hayloft or the woods. But all I see is a terrible darkness. Is it because he's nowhere except in my mind? No, he's too real. He *has* to be somewhere. I fill with dread.

"Jacky, where are you? Why can't I see you?"

"Because." His voice goes strange, like he's smiling. Only whatever he's smiling at isn't funny.

"What's wrong?"

"Nothing," Jacky singsongs. "I'm in my special place is all. No one can see me here. No one."

"What's your special place? *Where's* your special place?"

"Ask Arty. He knows. He's the only one who knows."

"No. I'm asking *you*. If you're my friend, tell me."

He doesn't say anything. *Why not? Is he scared? Playing games?*

I concentrate. Where is it so dark no one can see? The coal room, where I found his drawings? Someplace he and Mr. Sinclair played? Not the barn; light gets in through the cracks. But what about a place in the woods?

"Jacky, is there a cave near the boulders? Some underground hideout? Is that your secret place?"

A twig snaps to my side. *Who is it? What is it?* I don't want to find out.

I run.

# 24

'm at Main Street in no time. There are people and cars all around. Things are normal, at least to everyone but me. I won't sleep till I know what happened to Jacky.

I check my phone. Ten o'clock. There's time to go to the *Weekly Bugle* before I meet Mom for lunch. Now that I know Mr. McTavish died in June 1964, I can ask to get specific issues out of storage. Going back to March should cover the time from when Jacky and his mother disappeared and Cody's great-grandmother accused Mr. McTavish of murder.

The *Bugle* is in an old stone building with arched windows. A bell rings when I open the door. Ahead of me, a counter blocks off a wide aisle with office partitions on either side. Beyond them there's a printing press and rolls of newsprint stacked on heavy shelves.

"Hello? Anybody there?"

"You gonna get that?" somebody shouts from an office on the left.

"I'm busy, Gus," somebody else shouts from the right.

"You're always busy," Gus grumps and hauls himself to the counter. "What can I do for you?"

Gus is pretty gnarly, with a lumpy nose, a belly over baggy pants, and rolled-up shirtsleeves. His arms are like huge hairy sausages. Even his knuckles are hairy. You could make wigs with the stuff.

"I'm doing a history project for school. Could I please see some of the old editions in your archives?"

Gus looks at me like I've wandered in from Planet Simple. "Our archives?"

"Yes, please. I need to read the issues from March through June of 1964."

"Does this place look like a reading room?"

*Excuse me? I'm getting attitude from a guy who belongs in a circus?*

I smile the kind of cheesy smile I use to drive Mom nuts. "No, sir. I thought this was the *Weekly Bugle*. And I thought the *Weekly Bugle* might have copies of the *Weekly Bugle*. Because I thought the *Weekly Bugle* publishes the *Weekly Bugle*. Or maybe I'm wrong?"

Gus glares like I've made his hangover worse. "They're stored at the library."

The librarian is way nicer, maybe because I'm the first person she's seen in days. She takes me into what she calls "The *Weekly Bugle* Room" at the back. It's basically a floor-to-ceiling filing cabinet. Issues of the *Bugle* are bound by the month on wooden frames and hung in rows around the walls. At the center of the room is a large walnut table with a hard-backed chair on each side.

Ms. Browning—according to her name tag—finds what I'm looking for in about ten seconds. "Take all the time you need," she says cheerily and glances at my backpack. "Just a friendly reminder: no food or drink in the library, and cell phones off, please, and thanks."

I make a big show of turning off my phone and putting it in my no-food, no-drink backpack. Ms. Browning breezes out, leaving the door open. I'm not sure if this is to let in air so I can breathe, or so she can keep an eye on me. Who cares? All that matters is the murder.

Back in the sixties, issues were just twelve pages each. But with weekly issues from March through June, I still have nearly two hundred pages to plow through. I try to stay focused, but it's hard not to be distracted. For instance, there's this totally weird column you'd never see today called "It Says Here…" about who's coming to town to visit relatives, such as, "It says here that Mrs. Grace McKinnon will be serving a roast-beef dinner on Saturday, March 7, to her brother Mr. Clyde Waterston, sister-in-law Mrs. Bess Waterston, and nieces and nephew Wilma, Bonnie, and Fred Waterston, formerly of Wolf Hollow, now residing in Spruce Grove, Iowa. Save some for us, Grace."

Then there are the ads. The pharmacy has a sale on Brylcreem and other hair gunk; Kresge's is offering two-for-one hula hoops; and the Co-op has tractors you have to see to believe.

After taking forever with the first couple of issues, I force myself to stick to the headlines. Mostly they're things like: "Roller Rink to Open by End of April," but on the last page of the third week of March, I see one that makes my eyes pop.

## Local Man Reported Missing

Mr. Matthew Fraser has gone missing, according to his cousin, Mrs. Hannah Murphy. "Matthew disappeared two weeks ago," she told the *Bugle*. "Police Chief Cole has done nothing."

The police chief denies the allegation. "We contacted Mr. Fraser's former employer at Wolf Hollow Plumbing," he told the *Bugle*. "Mr. Fraser had notified his employer that he would be leaving town. It is a shame that he failed to inform his cousin of his decision. However, there is no reason to suspect that Mr. Fraser is in any danger."

*Oh my gosh. Mrs. Murphy! That must be Cody Murphy's great-grandmother! This is it!*

The next issue has a front-page photograph of Mrs. Murphy standing on an egg crate in front of the police station. She's yelling into a megaphone while hoisting a sign that says, "Justice for Matthew Fraser." She looks pretty crazy, like Cody when he punched me, and they have the same square jaw and bumps on either side of their forehead. The story reads:

## Accusations Lead to Arrest

Mrs. Hannah Murphy was arrested outside the Wolf Hollow police station Saturday, March 28, and charged with creating a public nuisance. She was demanding action in the matter of her cousin, Mr. Matthew Fraser, who left Wolf Hollow a little over three weeks ago.

Speaking into a bullhorn on the steps of the police

station, Mrs. Murphy accused Mr. Frank McTavish, a farmer on Guthrie Road, of involvement in what she termed her cousin's disappearance.

"McTavish's wife and son are missing too. Where are they?" Mrs. Murphy demanded. "What has he done with them?"

After taking Mrs. Murphy into custody, Police Chief Andy Cole told the crowd that neither Mr. McTavish's wife nor his son has been reported missing. He reminded those present that Mr. Fraser left town several weeks ago of his own accord.

Mrs. Murphy's husband, Mr. Reg Murphy, was unaware of his wife's protest and arrest until he was contacted by police. After a meeting with Chief Cole, the charge against his wife was dropped.

"Hannah hasn't been herself since Matthew left town," Mr. Murphy told the *Bugle*. "We look forward to hearing from Matthew, and ask that our family's privacy be respected."

Next issue, the case is on page two.

## Police Visit McTavish Farm

Police Chief Andy Cole and another officer dropped by Mr. Frank McTavish's farm on Guthrie Road last Thursday afternoon.

"We had no reason for concern," Chief Cole said,

"but made inquiries to reassure anyone who may have questions arising from last week's disturbance at the police station. Mr. McTavish welcomed us onto the farm. He reported that his wife, Mrs. Evelyn McTavish, left the area with their ten-year-old son, Jacky, three weeks ago. He said he had not filled out a missing persons report because he does not consider them missing."

Following an inspection of the property, Mr. McTavish gave police a letter that his wife had mailed him at the time of her alleged disappearance, postmarked Ramsay.

"Mrs. McTavish wrote that she and her son are traveling in the company of Mr. Matthew Fraser," Chief Cole said. "Given disagreements between herself and her husband, she has no wish to disclose her whereabouts. With her husband's agreement, we respect that decision."

Mr. McTavish told the *Bugle* that he is upset his wife has taken this unfortunate step, but that he will not seek a divorce as he hopes they may one day be reconciled.

"As for my son, I think of him constantly," he said, "but I believe it's in a child's best interest to be with his mother. When the time is right, I have no doubt he'll be in touch. Until then, with the burdens of the farm, I have neither time nor money to try to force his return, nor to raise him on my own."

The *Bugle* approached Mr. Ian Sinclair, neighbor to the McTavishes. "Every marriage has its ups and downs," he said. "The McTavishes are good friends and we wish them well." He refused further comment.

Police consider the departures to be a private family matter.

My head spins. If Mr. McTavish killed his wife, her friend, and Jacky, he'd have had to get rid of the bodies. The safest place would've been the farm. Anywhere else, he'd have risked being caught moving them. There'd also have been the chance of strangers finding them by accident. Anyway, they would have turned up by now. But if he buried them on the farm, why wouldn't the police have seen the dug-up ground?

So maybe everyone is right. Maybe Mr. McTavish *didn't* kill them. Maybe his wife just ran away with Jacky like Mom ran away with me. I mean, she wrote a letter.

*But why would Jacky say his mother left him behind? Why would he lie?*

My skin goes damp. Maybe there is no *he*. Maybe Jacky's just in my mind. I plow on. There's nothing in the next couple of issues. Then I turn to the last week of April.

## Hannah Murphy Charged with Trespass, Assaulting an Officer

Last Wednesday morning, Mr. Frank McTavish called police to report an intruder on his farm.

Upon arrival, Officer Angus Stebbing discovered Mrs. Hannah Murphy at the back of the property carrying a shovel. When he attempted to remove her, she struck him. She was charged with trespass and assaulting a police officer.

Mrs. Murphy told the *Bugle* that she'd gone to the McTavish farm to search for the bodies of Mr. Matthew Fraser, Mrs. Evelyn McTavish, and Mrs. McTavish's son, Jacky.

"Matthew had been seeing Evelyn for the past six months, and I don't care who knows it," she said. "He'd been planning to rescue her from a life of hell, but something happened. Matthew and I had no secrets. He would have contacted me. He's dead. They're all dead."

In an official statement, Police Chief Cole reconfirmed that the McTavish farm has been searched and that there is nothing to indicate foul play. "Mrs. McTavish, her son, and Mr. Fraser are traveling together and are at liberty to do so. Case closed."

Last night Mrs. Murphy was admitted to the Wolf Hollow County Sanatorium by her husband. She is currently resting.

Things get juicier in the next edition. There are two articles.

## Fraser Car Found

Police have found the car of Mr. Matthew Fraser, who

is believed to have left town six weeks ago with Mrs. Evelyn McTavish and her son, Jacky. The car, a 1948 Pontiac, was found nearby in Ramsay. It was parked on Elm Street, a block from the bus station. Ramsay was the postmark on Mrs. McTavish's letter to her husband.

"Mr. Fraser's car has been impounded. He has one month to claim it or it will be sold for scrap," said Police Chief Cole. "Our view is that Mr. Fraser drove his party to Ramsay to avoid being recognized in Wolf Hollow. From there, they proceeded by bus to parts unknown."

Ticket agent Mr. Harold Robinson reports that he may have seen the three, although he cannot be certain, given the many friends and relations who have passed through Ramsay over the last six weeks.

The second article comes with a pretty scary photograph of Mr. McTavish standing in front of the farmhouse with a dozen attack dogs.

## Farmer Buys Dogs for Protection

The *Bugle* spoke with Mr. Frank McTavish Friday afternoon at his farm on Guthrie Road. Mr. McTavish has been the subject of recent accusations by Mrs. Hannah Murphy, who is currently under observation at the Wolf Hollow County Sanatorium.

"I'm at my wit's end," Mr. McTavish said. "My wife took off with my son. As if that wasn't torment enough, I've been hounded by a crazy woman who has slandered me and trespassed on my property. I've had to get these dogs to make sure she stays clear."

When Mr. McTavish was asked what he knew about Mr. Matthew Fraser, the man currently traveling with his wife and son, he used words not fit for a family newspaper. "Matthew Fraser runs around the country with another man's wife, and his cousin Hannah Murphy wonders why he hasn't called her? Why, he hasn't the shame God gave a monkey."

In the event that his wife reads the *Bugle*, Mr. McTavish wants her to know that all will be forgiven if she returns, and that he loves and misses his son, Jacky. "In the meantime, these dogs are my comfort and protection."

There's nothing else for the rest of May or June. But there's a front-page headline at the beginning of July.

## Frank McTavish Killed by Dogs

Mr. Frank McTavish, a farmer on Guthrie Road, has been killed by his dogs. His body was found Wednesday. The county coroner's office believes he died sometime last week.

Mr. Ian Sinclair, neighbor to Mr. McTavish, made the identification. "There wasn't much to identify," he told the *Bugle*, "but I recognized what remained of Frank's shirt. Frank had kept to himself since his wife and son left him. We got concerned when our boy, Arty, asked why we hadn't been seeing Frank's cows out of the barn."

"We would have called," Mrs. Sinclair said, "but Frank had his telephone removed because of all the prank calls he'd been getting. And no one could go on that property since he got those dogs."

The Sinclairs contacted police when the dogs tried to attack their son in the woods that run along the back of their farm.

Upon arrival, officers destroyed the pack. Mr. McTavish's body was found inside his house. It is believed the dogs killed him when he opened the door to go outside.

Mr. Sinclair, executor to Mr. McTavish's estate, is attempting to locate the deceased's widow, Mrs. Evelyn McTavish, and their child, Jacky, who left the area in March.

Mrs. Hannah Murphy, whose cousin is believed to be traveling with Mrs. McTavish, remains in the county sanatorium and is unavailable for comment.

"Poor Frank," Mr. Sinclair said. "He got the dogs to protect himself, but nothing could protect him from the dogs."

# 25

Who knew old newspapers could be so interesting? Wow. I mean...*wow*! I'd give anything to talk to Cody's great-grandmother, but she's in the nursing home. How could I get to see her without getting into trouble?

Speaking of trouble, what time is it? I did into my knapsack and check my phone. Two o'clock. I'm dead. I dig into my knapsack. Mom's left a dozen messages:

12:15—What's keeping you?

12:30—Where are you?

12:35—Call me.

12:45—You're not at the rec center.

1:00—You're in big trouble, mister.

1:05—Please, Cameron, call. I'm worried.

No way I can just text. I race outside and phone her.

"Cameron!"

"I know, I know, I know, I know. I was in the library. I had to turn my phone off. I got distracted. Sorry. I'm really sorry."

"Library? What happened to the rec center?"

"I was doing research. I lost track of time. I'm sorry I ruined your lunch."

"You think I could eat? I was worried sick. You're still at the library?"

"Yeah."

"I'll be right there."

The Knotty Pine Inn is an upscale greasy spoon. It basically serves eggs for breakfast and burgers and specials for lunch and dinner, but it has checkered cotton tablecloths and menus with leatherette covers. Mom and I sit halfway back in a booth with red vinyl seat cushions and a fairly clean ketchup squirt bottle.

I know Mom's trying to be positive because she still hasn't yelled at me. All the same, she's way too quiet for comfort. In fact, she hasn't said anything. She's just listened to my nonstop apologizing.

Mom orders the chicken-salad-sandwich special, which comes with fries and a Coke. I order a cheeseburger and onion rings. As usual, she'll give me her Coke and half her fries.

"So," she says, after the waitress has left, "why were you researching at the library?"

"I had to look up stuff for my history essay."

Mom has a sip of water and puts the glass back in the exact water ring it came from. She's no good at acting casual. "I know you're interested in the ownership of the farm," she says carefully. "You weren't researching the Sinclairs, were you?"

"Not exactly."

"What do you mean, not exactly?"

I twist my water glass back and forth between my thumb and

fingers. "The Sinclairs came up in some of the articles, but sort of by accident."

Mom doesn't buy it. "Mr. Sinclair is our landlord. How he happens to have the farm is none of our business." She looks at me like I'm supposed to say "sorry" again. I don't. "You weren't planning on putting any of that in your essay, were you?"

"I guess not."

"Cameron. Promise me you won't say or write anything about Mr. Sinclair," she says, and starts in on her "character" speech, which manages to include why I mustn't rat out the Sinclairs and also why I need to be where I say I'll be and on time. It's full of words like trust, respect, privacy, loyalty, integrity, and responsibility, but mainly what I hear is *blah, blah, blah.*

Which is fine by me, because as long as I remember to nod and look serious, I can disappear in my head and think about more important stuff, like whether to believe Police Chief Cole or Cody's great-grandmother about the murders.

Chief Cole was probably right. Matthew Fraser told his employer he was leaving town, and since Mrs. McTavish was running out on a violent marriage, she had reasons not to say where she and her kid were going. Besides, Cody's great-grandmother looks nuts.

*Not so fast. Whacking a cop is pretty out there. But if I thought a cousin was murdered, wouldn't I do whatever it took to get the truth? Wouldn't I look crazy too?*

Yeah, but what about Mrs. McTavish's letter about leaving with Jacky?

*What about it? Mr. McTavish could've forced her to write it. He could've said he'd kill her if she didn't.*

Wouldn't she guess he'd kill her anyway?

*If I had a gun at my head, I'd do whatever and play for time. Besides, maybe he beat her till she wrote it or threatened to kill Jacky too. If Dad threatened to kill me, Mom would do anything.*

Okay. So she writes it, and when Matthew Fraser comes for her and Jacky, he kills all three of them.

*Right. Then he waits till night and drives Mr. Fraser's car to Ramsay, where he abandons it near the bus station, mails the letter, and walks home. He'd be back before sunrise. And when the car gets discovered, well, it's a '48, a junker. Everyone thinks they ditched it and disappeared on a bus.*

But Mr. McTavish would still be stuck with the bodies. If he'd moved them off the farm, they'd likely have been found by now. But the cops searched the property and said the ground was undisturbed. Plus it was March, so the ground was probably still frozen. So where did he put them? And what about Jacky? He says his mother left without him and that Arty saw him after she'd gone.

*So maybe his father just murdered Jacky's mom and Mr. Fraser, and let him live.*

But if Jacky was alive, why wasn't he found after the dogs killed his father? Even if the dogs got Jacky too, there'd have been bones, wouldn't there? That Davy Crockett cap at least?

"Cameron," Mom says, "who are you talking to?"

"What?"

The waitress puts our meals on the table. "There we are then. Enjoy."

"Thank you," Mom says without taking her eyes off me. The waitress disappears. "I was talking to you, Cameron," Mom continues, controlled and intense. "Suddenly your lips began moving like we discussed the other night. Where were you? Who were you speaking to?"

"No one. I was here. I was listening. You were talking about integrity and responsibility."

"What else?"

"Punctuality?"

Mom looks at me like she's a teacher and I've just failed a test and she's very disappointed. "You were talking to Mr. Sinclair, weren't you?"

"No."

"You were asking him how he got the farm."

"It wasn't about him at all."

"Then what?"

"You'll flip out."

"I won't."

*She will.* "Promise?"

"Promise." Mom presses her hands on the table so she can concentrate on not being upset.

"Okay. But remember what you said about trust." I take a deep breath. "You know that kid who hit me?"

"You were having a conversation with *him*?"

"No. His great-grandmother thinks that the man who used to have our farm, the man who got killed by his dogs—she thinks he murdered his wife, his kid, and his wife's boyfriend. I was asking myself stuff like whether he made his wife write a letter before he killed her and where he buried the bodies."

Mom stares at me like I'm an alien.

"You promised you wouldn't flip out."

"I'm not flipping out." Mom presses her fingers into the table so hard her nails turn white. "But you do know this is unhealthy, don't you?"

"You mean sick?"

"All right, sick. You take some old story, and instead of laughing it off—the normal thing to do—you act as if it's real, imaging violence and horror instead of enjoying a pleasant lunch in the here and now. It's disturbing, Cameron."

I bang my hand on the table. "See, this is why I never tell you stuff. You promise you won't freak out and then you do. It's not my fault I picture things or talk to myself. If I try to keep all the stuff in my head inside, I'll explode."

"Cameron," Mom says quietly, "please keep your voice down. The woman two tables behind you is staring at you."

I turn around. "Hey, was I talking to you?"

The woman cowers over her coffee like I'm going to attack her with a spoon or something.

"I'm sorry. He didn't mean that," Mom says to the woman and then zeroes back on me. "Cameron, we need to have a serious conversation, but not here, not now. Finish your burger. I have to get back to the office. I'll see you at five. Don't be late."

# 26

I'm at the office at ten to five. Mom finishes up, and we say good-bye to Ken and head home. I tell her I'm sorry about the restaurant stuff, especially being rude to that woman, and she says good, but don't let it happen again. Then she smiles and tells me she's pleased I was researching my essay. "That shows real initiative, only next time keep your eye on the clock."

I smile and nod and say whatever, but mostly I try not to think about the cemetery. I keep seeing the dog appear out of the mist and wondering about Jacky's dark, secret hiding place. It's like that all day. But that's better than what happens when I go to sleep. Tonight's nightmare is especially real.

I dream I wake up and someone's in my room.

"Who's there?"

"Shhh. It's okay, Buddy. It's only me."

Dad. I sit bolt upright. "Dad, what are you doing here?"

"I live here."

"Does Mom know?"

"Your mother's gone."

"Gone? Where?"

"Guess." Silence, except for the sound of him breathing. "I have a surprise for you."

"What kind of surprise?"

"You'll see." Now Dad's voice is in the hall. "Follow me, Jacky."

"I'm not Jacky. I'm Cameron."

"Whatever you say, son."

There's a candle on my bedside table. I light it. Shadows dart around my room. None of the things here are mine. Drawings of dogs are taped to the walls and ceiling. Something tickles my left ear—the tail of the raccoon-skin cap I'm wearing.

"This way," Dad calls.

I take the candle into the hallway. It's long and dark.

"This way. Don't be frightened, Buddy. I won't hurt you."

I follow Dad's voice down the hall for what seems like forever. At last, I get to the door of the big room over the kitchen and step inside. It's empty. The trapdoor to the attic is open. There's a ladder.

"I'm up here, Buddy."

I climb up into the darkness, holding the candle in one hand and steadying myself with the other. As I near the top, Dad reaches down and grabs me under the armpits. He hoists me into the attic and swings me around and around. "Is this fun, Buddy?" My candle goes out.

"Dad! Stop it!"

He sets me down. A kerosene lamp flares up; he's holding it in his hand. Only he's not Dad. He's Mr. McTavish. "Surprise."

I scream.

"Your mother didn't leave you after all." Mr. McTavish grins.

"Cameron!" It's Mom. Her voice is coming from behind me. I

whirl around. Only instead of Mom, I see Mrs. McTavish. She's taped up in plastic, hanging by her neck from a rafter.

"Cameron!"

I scream again—because there's another body, a man's, hanging next to her.

"Cameron! Wake up!"

All of a sudden I'm in my bed. The lights are on. Mom's shaking me. "Wake up, Cameron! Wake up!"

"Mom!" I hold her tight.

"Cameron!" She strokes my hair. "What on earth were you dreaming?"

"I can't remember."

That's a lie. I do, only I can't *say*: the truth is too scary. What I dreamed was more than a dream. It was a message from Jacky. He was showing me his hiding place. And how he and the others got there.

# 27

By morning things are clearer than ever. Mr. McTavish found out his wife was about to leave him for Matthew Fraser, the cousin of Cody's great-grandmother. He waited till Jacky was at school, then he made her write the letter saying she'd run off with Mr. Fraser and Jacky. After she wrote it, he killed her.

When Mr. Fraser came by, Mr. McTavish killed him too. He hid the car in the barn, taped the bodies in plastic and hung them in the attic. When Jacky got home, his father told him his mother had left. From now on, he said, Jacky wasn't to leave the farm or see anyone, or something bad would happen. Jacky was so scared of his father that he did what he was told. That night Mr. McTavish drove Mr. Fraser's car to Ramsay, mailed the letter, and was back home by sunrise.

Two weeks later, Cody's great-grandmother went bananas. The cops came by to shut her up. They didn't really investigate because they thought everything was normal. Mr. Fraser had told his boss he was leaving town, and Mr. McTavish had his wife's letter.

But Cody's great-grandmother didn't let up. Mr. McTavish got guard dogs to keep her away, but by then he must have realized Jacky wouldn't stay hidden forever. After all, Jacky's friend Arty lived just one

ALLAN STRATTON

farm over, and kids get nosy. Once Jacky was found, the truth would come out—so Mr. McTavish called Jacky up to the attic, where he killed him too. Seeing his mother and Mr. Fraser's bodies—that's the part Jacky won't talk about, the part he tries to block from his mind.

Anyway, now Mr. McTavish has three bodies taped up in the attic—Jacky's dark, secret hiding place where no one can see. He seals the trapdoor with nails and paint. That and the tape and plastic hide the smells of the corpses. Not that he has to worry. He's always been a loner—even his best friends, the Sinclairs, think he's strange—and with the guard dogs, nobody comes by.

Everything's perfect; Mr. McTavish has gotten away with it. But then one day, the dogs kill him when he opens the door to go outside. By the time he's discovered, people figure any smell is from what's left of him. The Sinclairs lock up the house and farm the land. By the time Mr. Sinclair moves in, it's ten years later and the bodies have all dried up.

And that's that. Until I saw Jacky. But who'll believe me? I could take a hammer and break into the attic to find the bodies, only what if I'm wrong? Mom already thinks I'm crazy. Maybe she'd put me in a mental home for my own good, like what happened to Cody's great-grandmother.

No. Before I say anything, I have to be surer than sure. And there's a way: the man hanging beside Mrs. McTavish in my dream had a broad forehead, a lean jaw, a dark brush cut, and clear blue eyes bugged wide in terror. There were no photographs of Matthew Fraser in the *Bugle*; the only place I've seen him is in my dream. So, if that's what he looked like, my dream was true.

And how to find out? By talking to Hannah Murphy, Cody's great-grandmother, that's how. Even when old people forget new stuff, they're supposed to remember things from long ago. Mrs. Murphy was very close to her cousin. She'd remember what he looked like for sure.

But how do I get to ask her? After all, it's not like I can just barge into her room at the nursing home. I have an answer for that too: Benjie!

Monday morning, Cody and his friends bark at me when I get on the bus, but they don't do much else. Even Cody's too smart to try something right after a suspension. When Benjie gets on, he asks me how I spent my time off, and I tell him it was great—nonstop TV and video games. Then I ask about his weekend, knowing he'll go on about spending another Sunday with his grandpa at the nursing home. Sure enough.

"I don't wanna sound harsh, but it was soooo boring and my church pants itched like crazy."

I nod and exhale solemnly. The first time I sigh, Benjie doesn't notice. So I sigh again and again, till you'd think I was trying for an Oscar for Best-Ever Performance of Being Upset.

"What?" he asks.

I suck in my breath like I'm hurting inside but being brave about it. "Mom thinks my grandpa can't take care of himself anymore," I lie. "She's been talking about moving him here and getting him put in that home. Only the way you make it sound…"

"Gee, sorry. Don't worry. It's a nice place. Really."

I shrug, all gloomy, and look at my shoes. "That's easy for you to say."

"Seriously, check it out."

"How?"

"Are you a dummy or what? Like I told you, I go after school on Wednesdays too and meet up with Dad when he finishes work. If you want, I could bring you with me, show you around. You could get your mom to drive you home after."

"Really? You'd bring me with you?"

"Sure. No prob."

*Mrs. Murphy, here I come.*

# 28

The next couple of days I'm up and down like a toilet seat. Once I'm at the home, how do I ditch Benjie to see Mrs. Murphy? What'll I say to her? What if she's not alone? Worse, what if Cody busts in while I'm there?

I try to talk about it with Jacky. No such luck. He watches me all around the house, but he won't come out. Like, he'll be at the door to my room, but when I look up from my desk, he's gone. Same thing when I'm in front of the TV. He'll be staring at me from behind the leather armchair in the corner, but when I go over to flush him out, he's vanished.

"What's the deal, Jacky?" I whisper, low enough so Mom won't hear. "I'm doing this for you, you know. If you didn't want me to, why did you send me that dream?"

Maybe I'm being too harsh. Hearing me talk about this stuff must be hard for him, especially if the closest he can get to facing the truth is to send me a dream.

By Tuesday, Mom's asking why I'm so jumpy.

"What do you mean? I'm fine," I say. *As if.*

But time's weird. Waiting to meet Mrs. Murphy felt like forever, but suddenly it's after school Wednesday and I'm heading to the nursing home with Benjie. He goes on and on about school and teachers and parents and girls and basically whatever's passing through his head. He just opens his mouth and words come out. That's mean, but I wish he'd shut up so I can concentrate on what's coming.

At the end of a couple of blocks we get to a large property with a fancy sign that says: Wolf Hollow Haven, A Community of Care.

"So, this is it," Benjie says.

I hesitate. "You think Cody could show up?"

Benjie sighs. "Relax. Cody mainly comes on weekends with his grandparents, on account of when he's alone, his great-grandma asks him to take her home with him. I've heard her begging in the hall and in the social room. It's pretty embarrassing. Don't tell him I told you or he'll kill me, but it makes him cry."

"Cody cries?" Somehow that makes me feel better.

We walk up the circular drive. The home is more or less modern, meaning it's not new enough to be fresh or old enough to be haunted. On the left, there's a gated garden with picnic tables and chairs where families can sit with their relatives when it's sunny.

"You have to punch in a code to open the gate, like at all the doors," Benjie says. "That's to make sure the crazy ones don't wander off."

"How do you remember the codes?"

"Easy. They're posted right near the keypads. When people are demented, they don't make the connection."

I shiver. Will I ever be in a place like this? I can hardly imagine being twenty. What about Mom? What about Grandma and Grandpa?

Benjie keys in the code. The glass doors slide open and we step into the lobby. Not bad. The ceilings are high. There's lots of light and potted plants; also a reception counter with a sign-in register, flowers, and a sleeping orange tabby that apparently goes by the name Mr. Muffin.

"Hi, Brenda," Benjie says to the receptionist as he signs in.

"You again," Brenda teases. "So what's up at school this week?"

"Not much. This is my friend Cameron. I'm going to introduce him to Grandpa. His grandpa may want to come here."

"He might like to see this," Brenda says and hands me a brochure.

"Thanks." I fold it in two, stick it in my back pocket, and go to sign in while Benjie pets Mr. Muffin. Wait. What if Cody comes by, sees my name, and wonders what I was doing here?

*Like Cody's really going to read a sign-in register. Don't be stupid.*

Stupid or not, I scribble my name so no one can read it, then Benjie and I walk down a corridor wide enough for wheelchairs to pass each other, and around people with canes and walkers or who just stand holding the handrail.

A woman Grandma's age marches toward us in a polka-dot blouse and track pants. "They're really something today, aren't they, but what can you do?" she says and keeps on marching.

"That's Margaret," Benjie whispers. "She thinks she works here."

We cross a large open area where old people sit on couches staring into space or at tables playing cards or in front of the TV beside the piano.

"They have art classes and sing-alongs here," Benjie says. "Oh, and that's the door to the dining hall and over there's the chapel.

And here's Grandpa's wing. Some people are with it; some aren't. The wings are mixed, except for Memory Lane, where they put the ones who've forgotten how to move or talk."

"Creepy."

"Yeah, but everything else is nice, huh? I mean, if you're old. Mom says the best thing is it doesn't smell of pee."

We walk down the hall. Most bedrooms are singles; a few, doubles. Beside each door are the person's name and a glass case with personal photographs and knickknacks, I guess to help people know which room is theirs. We pass Mrs. Hilda Green. Mr. James Hardy. Mrs. Hannah Murphy.

*Hannah Murphy.* My heart skips. There's a photo of Cody and his parents in her memory case. As we pass, I glance inside at a tiny woman in a robe looking out the window into the courtyard.

A few more doors and Benjie says, "This is Grandpa's room." His memory box has family photos, a plaque from the 4-H Club, and a small brass tractor replica.

Inside, Benjie's grandpa is propped upright on one of those adjustable hospital beds with guardrails. Benjie says hi and introduces me, and we pull up a couple of chairs. His grandfather raises his hand a few inches and makes sounds that I think mean, "Benjie, how are you? Good to see you," but it's hard to tell.

Benjie takes his grandfather's hand and talks to him. I feel totally guilty—guilty about being here pretending to be Benjie's friend and about the mean things I've thought about him. He's so kind. Would I visit my grandpa twice a week if he was here? I want to think so, but I'm not sure. That makes me feel bad too.

After a while, even Benjie runs out of things to say. We sit there with him and his grandpa just looking at each other. At last his grandpa makes a sound.

"TV?" Benjie asks.

His grandpa raises a finger, which I guess means yes. Benjie takes the remote from the night table and clicks on the TV at the end of the bed.

Now's my chance.

"I think it's probably time for me to be going," I say to Benjie. "Thanks for bringing me here."

"Sure thing," Benjie says, switching channels. "Don't forget to sign out."

"I won't." I turn to his grandfather. "Nice meeting you, Mr. Dalbert." His grandfather makes a sound. I'm not sure what he's saying so I just smile and nod. "Bye then."

"Yeah, bye. See you tomorrow," Benjie says, his eyes glued to the sports channel.

I back out of the room into the empty corridor and walk toward Mrs. Murphy's room as quickly as I can. At her memory case I get a panic attack. What am I doing? What if anyone finds out?

*Like who? Benjie's glued to the TV. He'll be there for the next hour till his dad arrives from work.*

What about staff?

*I'm signed in. If anyone sees me, they'll think I'm a visitor.*

What if Mrs. Murphy tells?

*Who says she'll even remember? Anyway, I can give her a fake name.*

But what if Cody shows up?

*What are the odds? Benjie says he only comes on weekends.*

How would Benjie know? It's not like he's here every day. Seriously, Cody would kill me. It's not worth it. Back out.

*No. This is the only way to know Mrs. Murphy's cousin was in my dream. If he was, the dream was real and there are three dead bodies in the attic. What's more important than knowing that?*

I knock gently and step into Mrs. Murphy's room.

# 29

Mrs. Murphy turns in her chair. Her hair is white and her face is covered in lines, but she still has a square jaw and bumps on her forehead like in the *Bugle* photo.

"What do you want?" she snaps. A bad temper sure runs in the family.

"I don't want anything. I just came to talk."

She grips the cane on her lap. "Who says I want to talk?"

"I'm a friend of your great-grandson Cody," I lie.

"Cody." A light goes on and she's all smiles. "You're a friend of Cody?"

"Yes. I came by to say hello for him."

"Oh… Well, come in, come in." Her hand twitches me to the chair beside hers.

I look around at her stuff—a lifetime in a room. A small coffee table, all covered with framed family photos; the quilt on the wall (did she make it?); the painting of a farm (was it hers?); and the old knit lamb doll on her pillow.

Mrs. Murphy squints at me like she's trying to remember who I said I was and why I'm here, but is embarrassed to ask.

"So, yeah," I say, helping her out. "I'm here to say hi for Cody."

"Cody. That's nice. He's a very special boy, isn't he? My little Cody."

"I like that picture you have of Cody in the hall. I'll bet he's in some of these other family pictures too."

"Oh, yes, I have lots of pictures of Cody."

"Can I see at a few?"

She nods, and I check the frames up close, pretending to see Cody while searching for the face I saw in my dream, the face of her cousin Matthew Fraser. He could be in one of those grainy, washed-out color shots from the early sixties or in a black-and-white photo from when he was a kid, maybe in a group of kids and cousins at a family picnic. Either way, it'll be hard to spot him.

"Those are great pictures," I say, sitting down again. "I really like the ones of you and your parents, kids, and grandkids." I have no idea if those shots are there, but it's a pretty safe bet. Also a safe bet that she won't disagree in case I'm right.

"So many children." Mrs. Murphy nods happily. "So many children."

"With all those children, you must have had a lot of cousins."

"Oh yes."

"Can you point them out to me?"

She thinks a bit. "I'm afraid my eyes aren't so good anymore."

I have another way to fish. "I have a favorite cousin," I say casually. "Did you have a favorite cousin?"

"I expect so."

"My favorite cousin is Aaron. Can you tell me yours?"

"Yes."

"Who?"

Mrs. Murphy pauses. "Oh, you know." She winks as if she's told me a joke and looks at me like it's my turn to say something. Why doesn't she say Matthew's name? Maybe she can't remember and doesn't want to let on.

I throw her a clue: "I hear you had a really great cousin called Matthew."

"Matthew." Her eyes cloud over.

"Yes, Matthew Fraser."

Mrs. Murphy puts her finger to her lips. "Reg says I'm coming home next week. I mustn't talk about Matthew."

Reg. The name of her husband in the *Bugle*. But I'm pretty sure he's dead. Does Mrs. Murphy think she's in the county sanatorium?

"Reg is right. We shouldn't talk about Matthew." I nod seriously. "But I'm pretty sure it's okay to say what he looked like."

"Well, Matthew looked like Matthew."

"I know. But could you describe him?"

Mrs. Murphy stiffens. "Why?"

"No reason." Time for a happy thought. "I know your great-grandson Cody. Your farm is just a bit farther from town than ours."

"You're on a farm near ours?"

"Yes. The one beside the Sinclairs."

"The McTavish farm!" Mrs. Murphy bangs her cane on the floor. "Frank McTavish killed Matthew!"

"Shhh. Please, Mrs. Murphy. Shh!"

She lurches to her feet and raises the cane. "Don't tell me to shush!" she yells. "I know what I know!"

I jump up and raise my hands. "It's okay, Mrs. Murphy. I know."

"Don't lie to me! Do you think I've lost my wits? I'm not crazy!"

"Mrs. Murphy, please!"

"Who are you anyway?" She takes a step toward me. "You're not a doctor!"

I back up. "I'm a friend of your great-grandson Cody."

"Liar!" She swings her cane. "Cody's a baby!"

"Mrs. Murphy, please. I'm just a kid who lives on the farm."

*"Jacky's the only boy on that farm! He's dead! They're all dead!"* She swings again. Her cane knocks the framed photos off her tea cart. They crash to the floor, and glass shatters. *"Who are you? Who sent you?"*

"Nobody!"

Mrs. Murphy charges toward me. I race into the corridor. To my right, Benjie is staring out of his grandpa's room, mouth wide open. Nurses and workers run down the hall from behind him. Others run up from my left. They pour past me into Mrs. Murphy's room.

The last one grabs my arm. "What were you doing in there?"

"Nothing!"

I shake free, and she falls as I bolt to the social room, cross it, and dash down the hall to the front doors by the reception desk.

"Don't forget to sign out," Brenda says cheerily.

No time. The nurse who fell is back on her feet and barreling toward me. I see the code by the door, tap the keypad, and escape as she bursts into the foyer.

"Stop. Come back."

*Are you kidding?*

# 30

I make it to Ken's office in no time.

"What are you doing here?" Mom asks.

"Didn't want to take the school bus. Thought I'd come by to say hi to Ken."

The idea I'd want to see Ken makes Mom so happy she forgets to ask why I'm sweating. "He's out showing a property, but he should be back soon." She thinks a sec, like she's wondering if the moment is right, then goes for it. "What would you say if we asked Ken for dinner? Nothing special. I could pick up some KFC and take a pie out of the freezer."

"Sure. Great."

It is too. If anyone calls about what just happened, Mom won't yell at me till Ken's gone. By then, she'll have had time to settle and I can give her a good story. Like, I went to visit Benjie's grandpa to be nice and ended up in Mrs. Murphy's room by mistake.

*Stop freaking. No one's calling. Our landline is unlisted on account of Dad, and anyway, the way I scribbled my name, who could read it? Even if Benjie rats to the home, by tomorrow things will have blown over.*

All the same, my stomach keeps churning. I try to forget what happened by pretending it was just a bad dream.

Ken's back at five to close up. As for dinner? "That'd be great," he says, like he's been waiting for this since forever. "I'll bring a bottle of wine."

We sit down to eat at six thirty. Soon it's seven thirty. Then seven thirty becomes eight. The more time passes, the more I relax. Okay, I shouldn't have been in Mrs. Murphy's room, but what did I do? Nothing. Just talked to her. Since when is talking to someone a crime? I mean, I'm not the one who smashed up her room.

I start to enjoy Ken's stories. He's not talking big or acting cool like he was at the beginning. He's more like when we were looking at that photo of his kids.

He tells a story about camping with his kids a few years back. It was his first time in a tent since Scout camp—he's not really into outdoor stuff—but he thought they'd like it. Anyway, he couldn't get the campfire going, so they ate a few cold hot dogs and marsh-mallows and went to bed. Only he forgot to put away the leftovers, not to mention the hamburger meat, and in the middle of the night some coyotes dropped by for a meal. So there he is, terrified they're going to come into the tent and eat his kids, and all he has to bash them with is his daughter's teddy bear.

"So how scared were you?" I grin.

"Let's just say it was a good thing I brought along an extra pair of underwear," Ken jokes. "I can't believe I was such an idiot. Not just to leave food out, but to worry about a few coyotes. Like I said before, coyotes are scared of people. I've been in the area fifteen years and only seen one a few times. But boy, that night I kept imagining the headline in the *Bugle*: 'Local family swallowed by coyotes.'"

We roar with laughter. I think, *You know, Mom could do worse.*

Out of nowhere, a car drives up to the house. Its lights are low.

"Expecting someone?" Ken asks.

Mom goes pale. She shakes her head. "Maybe it's Mr. Sinclair." But I know what she's thinking. Dad.

There's a knock on the door.

"Let me answer it," Ken says. His fist tightens, not much but enough in case there's trouble.

Mom nods. Ken opens the door. Two cops are standing outside. One's chunky, the other thin. Ken knows them. "Brian, George, what's up?"

"May we come in?"

"Of course," Mom says, scared and confused. "I'm Katherine Weaver." She shakes their hands. "Is this about my ex-husband? Is it about Mike?"

"No," says the heavy cop. "I'm afraid it's about your son."

I want to throw up.

"Cameron? Cameron, what did you do?"

"Nothing. I can explain."

"What do you mean, you can explain?"

"Perhaps if we could sit down?" the other cop asks.

Mom shows us into the living room. She sits between me and Ken on the couch. He squeezes her hand. The cops sit opposite us on the leather armchairs. The heavier one does the talking.

"We understand your son was suspended from school last week because of a fight with Cody Murphy," he says to Mom.

"I wasn't fighting. He was beating me up."

"Cameron!" Mom's glare shuts me up.

"This afternoon, Cameron went to the Wolf Hollow Haven nursing home. He was seen leaving the room of Mrs. Hannah Murphy, Cody's great-grandmother. Mrs. Murphy was visibly upset and needed restraint, in the course of which she received some bruises. Several of her framed photographs were smashed. When a nurse tried to detain Cameron, he knocked her to the ground. She twisted her ankle."

"Cameron?" Mom's eyes are wide in horror.

"It's not what it looks like."

"Does Cameron need a lawyer?" Ken interrupts.

"That's for you to decide," the thin cop says. "This is simply a warning visit. At this point, we don't believe there will be charges."

"Look," I say, "I was at the nursing home with my friend Benjie to see his grandfather. On my way out, I ended up in Mrs. Murphy's room by mistake. She went nuts on me, swinging her cane and knocking over her pictures. When the nurse grabbed me, I panicked and ran. I didn't mean for her to fall."

Silence.

The heavy cop looks right through me. "According to Benjie, you went to the home to check it out as a place for your grandfather."

"What?" Mom says. "Dad's in perfect shape."

"Benjie says you left him and his grandfather five or ten minutes before the incident," the cop continues. "That's an awfully long time to be in someone else's room by mistake. It's also a strange coincidence that it was the room of Cody Murphy's great-grandmother—Cody Murphy, the boy with whom you had the fight. We understand it started when you taunted him about his family."

"No. That's not how it happened."

The heavy cop turns to Mom. "It's no secret in town that Cody's had a rough go since his father died. The past few years, he's lived with his paternal grandparents and great-grandmother. He's very close to her. Last year she went to the nursing home. He's taken it hard."

"The poor boy," Mom says.

"Cody? Poor boy?" I exclaim. "He bullies everybody, and we're supposed to feel sorry for him? It's not fair!"

"The police aren't here because of anything Cody did," Mom snaps. "They're here because of you."

The thin cop takes out a notepad and points at me with his pen. "The nurse who twisted her ankle could have charged you with assault. Cody's family could have you charged on any number of counts. You could end up in juvenile detention. Luckily for you, none of them wants that. What they want is the truth. What were you doing in that room?"

What do I say? When I open my mouth this strange sound comes out, all gasping and choking at the same time. "I wanted to find out what her cousin looked like—Matthew Fraser. The man she said was murdered by Mr. McTavish, the owner of this farm in the sixties."

"Oh no," Mom says quietly. "Is this about your history project?" She turns to the cops. "He's been researching a history project about the farm."

"In the *Bugle*," I say. "It's all in the *Weekly Bugle*. Except Matthew Fraser's picture."

The cops exchange glances. "It's an old story," the thin cop tells Mom. "Back in the day, Mrs. Murphy claimed Frank McTavish killed his wife, his son, and Mrs. Murphy's cousin here on the farm. It turned out to be nothing more than a wife who ran off with her son and boyfriend."

"That's not true," I blurt out. "Mrs. Murphy was right."

"What do you mean?"

"Mr. McTavish killed them. Their bodies are in the attic."

# 31

Everyone's jaw drops.

"I'm sorry," Mom apologizes to the cops. "Cameron's always had an imagination. But this…this—"

"This is *real*, Mom. The bodies are taped in plastic, hanging from a rafter."

"You can't possibly know that," Mom says. "The trapdoor to the attic was sealed when we moved here."

"Check it out if you don't believe me."

"Cameron's right," Ken says. "I think we should go to the attic."

Yes! I could give Ken a hug.

"You're encouraging this?" Mom gasps.

"No. I'm saying Cameron believes what he's told us. Until he sees for himself that it's nothing, it'll be on his mind."

"But the door's nailed shut," Mom says, "and the nails are covered with so many coats of paint that we'll need a hammer and crowbar to break in. Think of the damage."

"I am," Ken says, with a nod in my direction.

*Gee, thanks, Ken. Guess I was wrong about you being my friend.*

Ken pulls out his phone and dials. He holds up a hand for us all to shut up. "Art, it's Ken Armstrong. I'm next door with Brian and

George from the station. Look, I know this sounds strange, but we need to get into your attic. Katherine's afraid there'll be damage opening the trapdoor. I'll pay for repairs, but I wanted your okay." He holds the receiver away from his ear; I'm guessing it's *not* okay. "Art, I'm sorry, I can't say why on the phone. But it's important, trust me… Thanks." He hangs up. "Art will be right over."

Mr. Sinclair drives up in his pickup, a stepladder and toolbox in the back.

"I'm afraid Cameron's let that research paper go to his head," Mom tells him. "He thinks Frank McTavish killed his wife, their son, and her friend and locked their bodies in your attic."

Mr. Sinclair gives me a look. "So, you're a guesser."

"No, sir, I'm a knower." *The only thing I don't know is what* you *know.*

Mr. Sinclair snorts and heads upstairs with his stuff. We follow into the big room and watch him set up under the trapdoor. I'm kind of scared, but at least for now nobody's talking about Mrs. Murphy.

Ken volunteers to do the grunt work, but Mr. Sinclair won't hear of it. He scoots up the ladder, pries out the nails with a chisel and hammer, and bashes open the hatch with a crowbar. I knew he was tough, but wow!

Mr. Sinclair comes down. "If this is a crime scene, you boys better go in first," he tells the cops, wiping sweat from his forehead.

The cops turn on their flashlights and go up. The beams scan the darkness. Silence. Mom puts an arm around me. Ken holds her hand. None of us breathes. They come down, all serious, and whisper with Mom, Ken, and Mr. Sinclair. Right, as if I couldn't handle what I just told them.

I stare up into the pitch black. *Sorry, Jacky, your hiding place isn't secret anymore. But I had to tell. I had to.*

The whispering stops. Mom steps forward. "Cameron," she says, like she's at a funeral, "would you like to come up with us?"

I nod. Heart pounding, I climb the ladder after the cops. Mom, Ken, and Mr. Sinclair follow.

"Have a good look," the heavy cop says when we're all in the attic. He shines his flashlight in all directions.

The attic is empty.

"No. It's impossible."

Mom grips my shoulders. "You see, Cameron? You see? It was all in your head."

"It wasn't!" I pull away. "The bodies, they were here. Somebody moved them."

The heavy cop has had enough crap. "Who? When? Where?"

"I don't know."

*Wait. In the barn Jacky said Arty knew he didn't leave the farm with his mother. In the cemetery he said Arty knew the secret place where he was hidden.*

I whirl on Mr. Sinclair. "But *you* know. You know Jacky was here too."

Mom's jaw drops. "Jacky?" Ken steadies her. "Who? What?"

"Jacky was the McTavish boy," Mr. Sinclair says. "I showed Cameron pictures of us playing when we were kids. He left with his mother. Never saw him again."

"That's not true."

"How would you know?" the skinny cop asks.

"I just do. Mr. McTavish must've figured he couldn't keep the bodies up here for long. He had to get rid of them."

"If you're so smart, tell us how," the heavy cop says. "No human remains have shown up around here as long as I've been alive."

"I know. He didn't bury them."

"What did he do then, Mr. Kid Detective?"

This is the most horrible thought I've ever had in my life, but it's the only thing that makes sense. I turn to Mr. Sinclair. "Your father was Mr. McTavish's best friend. He had a grinder. It would've been so simple. You *know*. Tell them."

"Oh my God, Mr. Sinclair. I'm sorry." Mom's breathing so fast I think she'll faint. She cries out to anyone who'll listen. "Cameron's father, he tried to kill me, and we've been on the run. Cameron's had dreams, he's mixed up in his head, he needs help, he's not well, he's—"

"Stop it, Mom! This isn't about Dad. You always blame Dad. Always. For everything. It's not his fault!"

"Enough!"

"No! It's not enough. It's never enough. No matter what I do, you think I'm crazy. You always have. Well, I'm not! If anyone's crazy, it's you!" I drop to my knees and bang my fists on the floor, then my head. Ken pulls me back. I fight him off.

The heavy cop locks me in a choke hold. I black out.

# 32

When I come to, Ken and Mr. Sinclair are gone. I don't ask where or why. I don't say "sorry" either. I don't say anything. *Why am I here? Why am I anywhere? I wish I could disappear forever.*

The cops get me down the ladder and onto the couch in the living room. I stare at the baseboard across from me. Mom's been crying; she goes to the kitchen with the thin cop. They talk quietly, while the other one stands in the archway, arms crossed, in case I do anything. Eventually Ken returns with an overnight bag and the cops leave.

"I'm going to set up a cot for Ken in the big room upstairs," Mom says. "He'll be staying here tonight."

"What? You're scared of me?"

"No, Cameron, I'm scared *for* you." She sits beside me and puts her hand on mine. I don't stop her, but I don't look at her either, just keep staring at the baseboard. "If you have another outburst like what happened upstairs, I'm not strong enough to stop you."

"So, like, do I call you Ken or Mr. Security Guard or what?" I say to Ken without looking up.

"I'm here to help," Ken says. "That's all. I care about you. We all do."

"Right."

"Ken's going to arrange an appointment for you with his family doctor," Mom says. "The doctor should be able to give you medication for your nerves until we can set you up with someone to talk to."

"You mean a shrink."

Mom pauses. "This is my fault, Cameron, not yours. I should have seen this coming long ago. These past few years have been so hard on you. I thought I was all you needed, but I was wrong. I'm sorry."

I hear what she's saying, but it's just words.

"The officers say there won't be any charges as long as nothing else happens. They think it would be a good idea for you to stay home for a few days. Do you have any classes with Cody? Are your lockers near each other?"

I shake my head.

"Good. They say it's best if you see him as little as possible."

*Yeah. After all, I'm a freak, right? Like I could beat up a guy like Cody. As if.*

"Ken's canceling his appointments for tomorrow. He'll be here with you while I figure out things with the school. I'll see your teachers and get work for you to do so you don't fall behind. I'll also speak to your history teacher and have him cancel that essay about the farm."

"There is no essay," I say quietly.

Mom catches her breath. She's about to say something, but Ken must've caught her eye because she doesn't. "We'll get through this," is all she says.

I get ready for bed, and Mom comes in to say good night. She turns on a night light, reminds me Ken's down the hall if I need anything, and gives me a kiss on the forehead. "I love you."

I stare at the ceiling. "Mm-hmm."

She leaves. I hear Ken and her setting up the cot. It's not very comfortable; he must really like her. I hear the stairs creak as she goes downstairs to her room, and then I hear Ken settling in. Everything goes quiet. I lie still for a very long time.

*Jacky, why weren't you there? Where are you?*

Silence.

Maybe Mom's right. Maybe I *am* crazy.

Mom checks on me in the morning; I pretend to be sleeping. I ache all over. There's a nasty bump on my forehead and my arms are bruised. I really banged myself up last night.

I hear Mom and Ken talking in the kitchen, and I'm pretty sure it's about me. Mom leaves before eight. She probably wants to see the principal first thing. When I finally come down, Ken gets me corn flakes and grapefruit, the whole time talking about the weather like nothing happened last night and it's not totally weird he's here.

"You like coffee with milk, right? And lots and *lots* of sugar?" He winks.

Me and that cappuccino machine. I don't feel like smiling, but I do. "Not really."

He watches me eat. "Want anything else? Living on my own, I know how to make bacon and eggs. I'm also pretty good at takeout."

I shake my head. It's hard, but I have to say it: "I'm sorry about the attic."

"That's okay."

"I hope Mom knows."

"Absolutely. She loves you."

I have to focus on my toast or I'll lose it. "I was so sure."

"I've been sure about lots of things that didn't turn out the way I expected. Nothing wrong with that."

I think for a long time. "There's a reason I thought what I thought."

Ken smiles. "There's always a reason why we think things." He's not going to ask. He's going to make me say it.

"Promise you won't tell Mom?"

"I can't promise that. But whatever it is, she'll understand."

"She won't."

"Well, *I* will."

I look in his eyes, and he looks right back. Okay, here goes. "A few nights after we got here, I thought I saw a kid looking out from the hole in the hayloft. I knew there'd been a boy who lived here years ago because of the stuff in the basement. I found his drawings in the coal room. His name was Jacky. Want to see them?"

"Sure."

I take Ken up to my room and show him the pictures.

Ken frowns. "I'm no expert, but this boy sure doesn't seem like a happy camper."

"No kidding. I knew the story about Mr. McTavish and the dogs from school. And see how his mom disappears from his drawings? And the dogs and the pitchfork and the blood and all?"

I pause. Ken nods, not like he's judging, just listening, waiting for me to go on. So I do. "Anyway, what with all of that, I started to wonder if Mr. McTavish had killed her, and if maybe the kid I thought I'd seen was Jacky's ghost or something. Especially after I heard how Cody's great-grandmother thought Mr. McTavish killed not just Jacky's mother, but Jacky and her cousin too. So I started to research. And I got that stuff from you and the *Bugle*."

"And things got bigger and bigger in your head until last night."

"Yeah. But even before that. Way before. I mean, I've been hearing his voice, sometimes just in my head, other times like he's beside me."

Did I actually say that? Ken keeps on nodding, like what I've said makes total sense. "I can understand why you were so upset."

"You can?"

"One of the many things I like about you, Cameron, is that you care about people. You try and imagine yourself in their shoes. So I'm not surprised you'd feel for the boy who made these drawings, imagine how he'd look and sound."

"But I do more than that. I talk to him, Ken. All the time. Mom says my lips move. She's right. Sometimes I catch myself."

That part's harder for Ken, but he doesn't laugh. "I think we all talk to ourselves. Maybe we don't talk out loud or move our lips, but when things are important, we imagine what we're going to say or what we should have said."

"Not to a ghost."

"No, maybe not. But I'm not God. There are lots of things I don't know or don't understand. Maybe it's only because I've never been through them." He gives me a fatherly pat on the shoulder. "You're a good kid."

"Thanks." Before we get up, there's something I have to say. "I'm glad you and Mom are friends."

I'm playing video games upstairs when Mom gets back. She has a word with Ken, then calls me to the living room. She looks like hell.

"For the rest of this week you'll be coming to town and doing your schoolwork at the realty office. I can't have you here alone. Ken's agreed to stay overnight till we know things have settled down. Next week you'll be at school on probation. The Murphys are very upset, but they've agreed with the principal that you can attend class if you don't speak to Cody; you have your lunches in the guidance office, not the cafeteria; and you don't take the school bus. I'll drop you off in the morning, and you'll report to the office at the end of each day, where you'll wait till I pick you up after work. Finally, there are to be no more video games."

"What?"

"Cameron, this isn't a conversation. It's what's happening. You'll be seeing Ken's doctor this afternoon. I'll be asking him to refer you to a therapist, for reasons that should be obvious. Cameron, talking to imaginary friends. To ghosts."

I whirl on Ken. "You told her!"

"I had to."

# 33

The rest of the week is the loneliest time of my life. I see Ken's doctor, who gives me prescriptions for sleeping pills that he calls muscle relaxants and for an antidepressant that he says should kick in after about ten days. Wolf Hollow is too small to have a shrink—or for anyone to want to be seen going to one—but he sets me up with one in Ramsay. She's too busy to see me right away, but she'll squeeze me in if there's "another episode."

Aside from seeing Ken's doctor, I'm stuck at the real estate office doing homework in a storage room. There aren't any windows, so it's like being in solitary. Mom said I could work up front near her, but that would be worse. Everyone coming in would wonder why I wasn't at school. At least if I'm hidden, we can pretend I've been sick. Which is actually what Mom thinks, only she means it like sick in the head.

That's the other reason I chose the storage room and to stay in my bedroom when we're home. Every time Mom looks at me, it's like she wants to cry. "I'm so afraid he's turning into his father," she said to Ken two nights back. She thought I was upstairs, but I was listening from the back stairwell. If she'd found out, she'd have said that proved it, that I was turning into a stalker like him.

Mostly I lie in bed and stare at the framed photo on my night table of Mom and my grandparents. I imagine the snapshot of Dad hidden underneath. Does he look like I remember? I want to know so bad, but what if, when I see his face, I get this overwhelming need to call him? A need where I can't stop myself? I mean, his number's on the back. It's right *there*.

I think about Dad a lot. There's not much else to think about, besides how I don't have any friends or anyone to trust, or how maybe I'm crazy like Mom thinks.

I mean, Jacky. What was that about? A few days ago I gave up asking him why he'd lied to me and gotten me in trouble. I gave up because, well, I was just talking to myself. He never said anything. I mean, it was like he wasn't there. And maybe he wasn't. Ever. After all, what did I know about him that I couldn't have guessed from seeing the stuff in the basement, his drawings, Mr. Sinclair's photographs, or the articles in the *Bugle*? Or that I might have made up because of stuff that happened with Mom and Dad or dreams that felt real?

If I made up Jacky, what else did I make up? That's what I wonder when I think about Dad. Like, what if the Dad in my head—the one my mom warns me about—isn't anything like my real dad at all? What if the fears Mom has about him are things she's blown up, like I blew up things I heard about Mr. McTavish?

Like that time he abandoned me in the middle of nowhere. What if it just seemed like the middle of nowhere because I was little, but it was really a park, and for *him* we were just playing hide-and-seek? Or that time he held me underwater. Maybe it *was* training.

After all, I can hold my breath the length of a pool now, can't I? Or that Facebook thing. What if he just missed me and it was his only way to find me? Mom's kept him away for years. What other choice did he have? Maybe she *made* him do it. Maybe it's *her* fault. And about that time on the balcony—he would never have dropped me. He was just playing airplane. Lots of dads do. Maybe I've remembered things all wrong.

When I think that, I hate myself for blaming him about things that aren't his fault. Then I hate myself for doubting Mom. I'm a bad son to Dad, to Mom—what's wrong with me?

# 34

*What's wrong with me?* That's what I'm thinking again tonight, Sunday night. Tomorrow it's back to school—to Cody who wants me dead and Benjie who ratted me out and a world of everyone staring at me and whispering about me. Tweeting about me too, I'll bet.

Anyway, it's late. I'm supposed to be sleeping, but I can't. I'm at my desk, looking out my bedroom window. It's pretty bleak. The fields are chopped, the leaves are down, and the sky is nothing but clouds. After dark, all you can see is a gray spill of light from the barn that catches the edges of the fields. Tonight's worse. The air is freezing into snow sand. When the wind whips it against the windowpanes, the sound makes me tighten the blanket around my shoulders.

Dad. Mr. McTavish. The dogs. If I let myself, I could picture the dogs looking up at me from the field. I close the curtains and hear a little voice behind me. "Cameron?" I'll bet Jacky's sitting on the edge of my bed, but I don't turn around. I'm afraid I'll see him.

"Cameron? Are you mad at me? Why won't you look at me?"

What do I tell him? That I'm afraid he isn't there?

"I know I haven't been around. I'm sorry, but I've been hurting. You said things about me."

I bite my lip and close my eyes. I see Jacky on the inside of my eyelids. "Before I talk to you again," I whisper, "you have to answer some questions."

"Okay." He looks nervous.

"Where are you when you're not with me?"

Jacky pauses. "I don't know."

"What did you do before I came?"

"Why are you asking me that?"

"Because people think I'm crazy. Sometimes *I* think I'm crazy."

"You're not," Jacky says. "I'd tell you if you were."

"But what if I am and you're just..."

"I'm me, Cameron. I'm just me. Jacky."

"No, you're something else," I say. "You pretend to be my friend, but you tell me things that aren't true, things that get me in trouble."

"Like what?"

"You know what—that your father killed your mother and her friend and hung their bodies in the attic; and that he called you up there and killed you too; and it's been your dark, secret hiding place ever since."

"I never said that. See, that's why I stayed away. You told everyone lies about Father and me. I didn't see any dead bodies. Not anywhere, ever. I never said I did either. That was plain horrible."

"Come on, Jacky. Those things were all in that dream you sent me."

"There you go, lying again. I never sent you a dream."

"What?" It's like I've been kicked in the gut. But it's true. I *guessed* he sent that dream, but it's not like I *knew*.

Hold up. Have I been talking loud? I get up from my chair and check the hall in case Mom or Ken is listening in, but the hall's empty. Ken's snoring lightly from his room. I close the door, prop myself up against my pillows, and shut my eyes. Jacky's cross-legged at the foot of the bed, winding the tail of his cap around his fingers.

"You're right. I'm sorry," I say quietly. "So what *did* happen when your mother left?"

His face crinkles up. "I don't want to say. It's hard."

"Please? I'm your friend."

"Okay, but don't tell." He looks down. "Father wanted Mother and me to be good. I didn't always listen though, so sometimes after I got the belt, he'd have to put me in the coal room for a day or so until I'd learned my lesson."

"You made the lines I saw on the wall?"

Jacky nods. "One for each time I was in there."

"That's awful."

"That's what Mother said, but she was wrong. It served me right. Mother gave me a flashlight and paper and crayons for if I got bored. I liked drawing there, seeing the colors in the dark. It's where I kept my drawings, even when I didn't have to."

"And your father called that teaching you a lesson?" I'm still unable to believe my ears.

"Uh-huh." Jacky nods. "Mother had to have lessons too. Only she never learned. One Saturday Father went to an auction. I saw Mother packing a suitcase. I asked her what she was doing. She said I'd find out soon enough."

I remember the times Mom's packed our bags.

"Father came back early. He said he knew what she was up to and told me to go to the attic and not come down till he said. I liked the attic. It was far away from downstairs, and when I was there, I couldn't hear them fight so much."

"When Mom and Dad fought, I used to stick my fingers in my ears and hum," I say.

"That works pretty good, huh?" Jacky gives me a shy smile, then gets all serious again. "After a while I didn't hear Mother yelling anymore and I thought maybe I could come down. Only a car drove up and there was a knock at the door. Then I heard a man yelling at Father."

Matthew Fraser, I think, come to take Mrs. McTavish and Jacky away.

"Mother's old hope chest was in the attic," Jacky continues. "I crawled inside and closed the lid and covered my ears and everything went away."

"Forever?"

"No. Until Father came and brought me downstairs. He sat me on his lap and stroked my hair and told me he had some bad news. Mother didn't want us. He said he'd tried to convince her to stay, but she'd left with her friend and wouldn't be coming back. He said for me not to worry. He loved me and we'd be happy, just the two of us, only I'd have to be extra good and stay inside from now on. He said if people knew I was on the farm without a mother, they'd take me away and lock me up in an orphanage."

"That's not true. They wouldn't."

Jacky's cheeks flush. "Are you calling Father a liar? You're the liar."

"You're right. I'm sorry." I wait till Jacky calms down. "So then what happened?"

"Father took the shovel from the back shed and said he'd be working in the barn for the rest of the day and I wasn't to disturb him. 'You stay inside,' he said."

"Did you?"

Jacky looks away. "I was supposed to."

"But *did* you?"

He shakes his head. "An hour later I looked out the kitchen window and saw Arty crossing his field to the woods. It was early spring; everything was in the ground. I wanted to tell him not to worry if he didn't see me, that I was okay."

"So you went to the clearing?"

"I made him swear to keep my secret or I'd be in big trouble. He did too. I could always count on Arty."

"Did anything else strange happen that day?"

"Late at night Father stuck his head in my room. I pretended to be asleep. A few minutes later he went outside. I heard a car. I peeked out my window and saw a car coming out of the barn. I didn't know whose it was. It drove away. Father was gone. I didn't understand. I was scared. But he was back by morning."

I think a bit. "Do you remember any people visiting the house after that?"

Jacky shivers. "A couple of weeks after Mother left, Father saw the police coming from down the road. He called for me to run to the barn and hide in the loft while they looked around. I buried myself in the hay. It was itchy. I thought I'd sneeze. But they were in and out of the barn in no time and everything was fine."

"But it wasn't fine, was it, Jacky?"

His eyes well. "Father got the dogs to keep people away. To keep us safe. But the dogs…the dogs…" He sobs. "It was my fault. All my fault."

"What was your fault?"

There's a knock on the door. "Cameron?" It's Ken.

Jacky disappears.

"Everything's fine." I get up and open the door. "I was just waking up to pee."

"Okay then." I can tell Ken doesn't believe me, but he goes back to bed, while I head to the washroom.

I know so much more now. Jacky definitely didn't leave with his mother. That's proof that the letter she wrote about him being with her was fake. There goes Mr. McTavish's alibi. He killed her and Matthew Fraser while Jacky was curled up in the attic hope chest.

*But what did he do with the bodies?*

Duh. Jacky said he took a shovel to the barn. He buried them in the dirt floor of the stalls, the one place where the ground was warm enough not to be frozen. The cows plodding back and forth packed the earth hard and stopped the stench—that and the hay bedding full of pee and cow pies. Add cops who didn't think there was a crime to begin with, and Mr. McTavish dug graves to last forever.

*Only what about Jacky? What happened to him? Why does he say he's to blame for his dad and the dogs?*

Until I find out about Jacky and the dogs, I can't say a word to anyone. Even then, who'll believe me after what happened in the attic? I wish I could go digging on my own, but there are more than a dozen stalls, and Mom and Ken would catch me before I got anywhere. Gee, that'd look good.

So what do I do?

# 35

What I do is stay up all night. Mom drives me to school. We arrive before the buses so I don't have to see anyone. The principal tells us I'm officially an "at risk" student—not at risk of getting beaten up, but for being "troubled." He lays down the law about me being in the guidance office when I'm not in class and sends me to English after the announcements.

There are a few snickers when I walk in. Mr. Bradley tells everyone to settle down. I'm guessing he knows what's going on. The principal probably sent a memo to the whole staff, or else they heard about it over the weekend. After all, it's not like anything's secret in this town, except murders.

Mr. Bradley has me sit in the front row to keep an eye on me. Then he has us turn to chapter six of *To Kill a Mockingbird* and asks a few questions about Scout's character, and life goes on.

Only it doesn't. Everyone's staring at the back of my head. They're passing notes about me. I can feel it, just like I feel the odd spitball when Mr. Bradley's back is turned.

It's like that all day. At lunch, kids watch me through the window of the guidance office like I'm an animal at the zoo. I don't see Cody, but his buddies wander by on his behalf. One points at his eyes and then at me, and mouths, "You're dead." I see Benjie too. He's the only one who doesn't look in, just walks straight down the corridor like I don't exist.

After school, when the guidance office is locked up, I wait on the bench in the main office till Mom arrives to pick me up. I'm going crazy thinking about what Jacky told me and about the bodies buried in the barn, but mostly about Cody and his gang. They're going to get me. But when? Where?

It's been like that ever since. Two weeks of being a nutbar nobody talks to, but everybody talks *about*. Two weeks of Cody's friends tripping me on the stairs, elbowing me into lockers, and muttering in my ear about how I'm going to get it one day when no one's around. Oh yeah, and someone scribbled "Cameron Weaver Is a Dickhead" on my locker with a Sharpie. The custodians got some of it off, but enough's left for everyone to see and laugh at.

There've only been two changeups in the routine. Kids don't bother making crazy signs at me in the halls anymore. They just move against the lockers on either side when I go by. I'm like Moses in that Sunday school story and they're the waters parting. Also, Ms. Adams, the guidance counselor, makes me eat lunch in her conference room. She says she felt bad, me being on display by the main window, but it's really to make it easy to lock me inside if I start "acting out."

Waiting for Mom after school is a bit better. So many kids are bused that the place is deserted, except for a few sports going on in the gym. It's boring though, and if Mom's late, the school's closed and I'm locked outside alone, freezing my butt off. I've told Mom about the threats from Cody's gang, but she says he wouldn't be stupid enough to try anything on school property. "Besides, you have me on speed dial," she says.

"Like that's going to help if Cody drives up and they haul me away in a car."

"Don't be silly," she sighs. "Cody's too young to drive."

"You think he cares?"

"He's not about to get himself arrested. That's crazy talk."

So it's normal for her to think Dad wants to kill us, but it's nuts for me to think Cody could drive a car. Who's crazy?

Anyway, before history one day I try talking to Benjie.

"Go away. I've got nothing to say to you. You lied to me. You used me. You got me in trouble." He walks off so fast you'd swear he was in a foot race.

"Please, I'm sorry," I say, keeping up.

"Too bad. Stop following me. I don't want anyone to see us talking. It's bad enough I sat beside you on the bus."

Home is no better. Jacky's back to hiding, too freaked by what he told me, I guess. I wish I could figure out his hiding place. That leaves Mom and Ken as the ones who'll talk to me—oh, and Grandma and Grandpa on our weekly happy calls, which are too weird to count as talking.

Ken tries to keep things light, but Mom watches me like a hawk. I'm surprised she doesn't make me use a plastic knife and fork in case I try to stab them, or wear foam padding for if I toss myself out a window.

Speaking of Ken, the only time he's been away was the weekend he drove the two hundred miles to see his kids. Is Mom really that scared to be alone with me?

"Kimberley's dance recital was amazing. I'll show you the video," he said when he got back. "Patrick's just started Cub Scouts, and he's already got badges for knots and walking the balance beam." Right, like they should be in *The Guinness Book of World Records* or the Olympics or something. Then he got quiet and sad, and Mom went all sympathetic.

I wonder if Mom wishes *I* were Patrick or Kimberley. I mean, they're obviously superhuman wonder-kids, and I'm a psycho nut-job who needs to have an unofficial guard around, since I'll obviously be too much for Mom to handle when I try to burn down the barn or start devil-worshipping in the basement.

Seriously, how long is Ken staying here? I mean, he's a nice guy and all, but it's not like I can trust him. And the longer he stays, the more it seems like Mom really *is* afraid of me.

"I'm worried he's turning into his father." I'll never forget her saying that to Ken. I know she's thought it once in a while, but to actually say it to someone besides me…

Dad. What if I *am* turning into him? Would that be so bad? Really? Once upon a time Mom loved him so much she married him. So how could he be *that* bad? Okay, maybe he messed up, and maybe I don't know all of it. But everyone messes up, don't they? I sure have. Mom has too, I'll bet. Or maybe Mom's God. She's sure been acting like it.

Besides, Mom doesn't know what Dad's like now. People change. That's what she's always told me: "It's never too late to change."

At that government place, Dad said he'd stopped drinking. And drinking was when the trouble happened. Okay, maybe not all of it, but most of it—at least the worst of it, the stuff I saw. That's what I remember anyway.

Ken's not perfect either. If he was, why did his wife get rid of him? Maybe it was just a bad match—but maybe that's all it was with Mom and Dad too. At least Patrick and Kimberley get to see Ken. Their mom doesn't hide them away and make them think their dad's a monster.

*Dad.* I lie in bed and stare at the framed picture on my night table, with the shot of him hidden underneath. *Dad, what would you say about all of this? Would you act like I'm a psych case? You sure couldn't treat me worse than everybody else does.*

All of a sudden, I get this need. I grab the picture frame and twist the clips on the back. The cardboard backing slides out—and there it is—the photo of Dad and me at the beach. We've made a sand castle—a pretty good one, with a moat and a wall—and he has his arm around me.

My heart races. I remember that day. It was one of our best days ever. Mom read on a beach blanket while Dad and I buried each other in sand. Then we all had soft ice-cream cones dipped in chocolate, and I got to try flippers and a snorkel mask.

Dad. He's laughing. So am I. We're happy. I flip the picture over. There's his number. He's a call away.

*No. I can't.*

Why not? I get that I can't see him. And I get that I can't let him know where I am. But just to hear his voice. To know he cares about me. Even just to know he's still alive. And to let him know I haven't forgotten about him. What's wrong with that?

I mean, there's got to be someone I can talk to. Who else? I can't talk to Mom. I can't talk to Ken. I can't talk to anyone at school. I can't even talk to my grandparents, not about real stuff. As for old friends, do I have any? It's not like I know them anymore. That leaves the shrink I'm supposed to meet, but no way I'm telling a stranger stuff I'm afraid to tell myself. No. Besides Mom, the only person in the whole world who *really* knows me is Dad.

Dad. I have to talk to Dad. I mean, if I can't talk to my own dad—I gulp for air. My skin tingles. I pull out my phone.

*No. Stop. Talking to Dad's not that easy.*

Why not? I have an unlisted number. Mom's made sure it doesn't show up when I call out.

*But she pays the phone bill. She won't look at local calls, but long distance? To Dad's number?*

By the time the bill comes, it'll be too late. We'll have already talked.

*So? She'll know. Think she's upset now? Just wait.*

Okay. So what do I do? Borrow one?

*From who? No one'll lend me a phone for long distance. I can't use a pay phone either. Dad would see the number and track down the area code. Besides, Mom and the school watch me twenty-four seven except in my room.*

Wait. I've thought of a way.

The next day, I see Benjie in the halls. "I need a favor."

"Not from me."

"Yes, from you, and I'm getting it."

"No way." He takes off on his speed walk.

I stay on his ear. "You ratted me out at the nursing home. But I didn't rat you to Cody."

"What do you mean?"

"He beat on me because I didn't tell him you were the one that told me about his great-grandmother."

Benjie ducks into the boys' washroom. I follow. We're alone.

"Look," he says, all pale, "I hardly said anything."

"What about her plowing into the church and leaving her car on the highway and almost burning down the house? You were laughing your ass off. What did you call her? Demento. A total whack job."

"That's not how I meant it."

"Think Cody will care?" I give Benjie ten bucks. "At lunch you're going into town to the drugstore. Get me a calling card for anywhere in North America. Slip it to me in math. If I don't get it, don't blame me if Cody taps on your shoulder."

# 36

After dinner I go upstairs while Mom and Ken watch some stupid TV show. I take out my phone and the photo of Dad and me, and stare at his number and the code on the calling card Benjie got me. The minutes will count as local. If Mom checks the bill and gets nosy, I can say I used the card to phone a kid I used to know.

I hold my finger over the keypad. I freeze. What's wrong with me? Dad is a touch tone away. What am I scared of?

I dial. The phone rings. Not just any phone. Dad's phone. After five rings I get worried that maybe he's changed numbers, but on the sixth he picks up. "Hello?" It's his voice, just like I remember it.

"Hello?" Dad says again, like he's wondering if there's been a wrong number and the other person's hung up.

*Say something.*

What?

*Something. Anything. "Hey, Dad" or "Hi, Dad"—something simple like that.*

"Is anybody there?" Dad asks.

I picture him frowning. I go to say hi, but the word sticks in my throat.

I hang up.

*Great. Just great.*

No big deal, I'll try again. Hearing Dad's voice—I was stunned is all. It's the first time I've heard it in years.

I dial. Dad picks up after four rings.

"Yeah?" Not so friendly, but not pissed off either.

"Uh...uh..." *Say it. Say it.* "Hi."

"Who is this?" It's like he thinks he should know but isn't sure. Why would he be? Last time he heard me, I was little. My voice was high and chirpy.

"It's..."

"Cameron?" Mom calls from the foot of the stairs.

"I gotta go," I tell Dad and shove my phone in my pocket like I've been caught at a crime scene. I go to my door. "What?"

"Ken's brought some dominoes. Want to play?"

"No, thanks. I'm going to bed."

"So early?"

"Yeah. I'm kind of tired. The pills."

"Suit yourself." I hear her wander off, saying something to Ken.

I close my door and pull out my phone. Should I call again? Dad may think I'm a crank. Or, next time, Mom may catch me.

*Relax. Mom and Ken are playing dominoes, probably at the kitchen table, other end of the house. And if Dad doesn't pick up, I can call tomorrow.*

I go for it. This time Dad's there on the first ring.

"Buddy?"

Did he hear Mom call my name? Did he guess? Whatever, he

knows. It's like he can see me, my room, everything. I go sweaty. This is it.

"Buddy, is that you?" Dad sounds like he wants it to be, but he's afraid to hope. "Buddy. Don't hang up. Please. I'm here. It's you, right?"

I swallow. Can he hear my breathing? "Yeah. It's me."

"Cameron! Buddy!" Suddenly his voice is bright and clear.

I flash on when I was maybe two, playing peekaboo. I had the covers over my head and Dad was going, "Where's Cameron? Where's my buddy Cameron?" I pulled the covers off my face, and he clapped his hands and went, "Cameron! Buddy!" like I'd appeared by magic. Which, now, I sort of have.

"I always knew you'd call, Buddy." He chokes up a bit. "I didn't know when, but I knew. You and me, we were always pals. Best pals. You were the greatest kid in the world. Still are. I love you, Buddy."

"Dad…I'm sorry it took so long."

"No. It's okay. You're on the phone now. Where are you?" He catches himself. "No, don't tell me. You'll get in trouble."

"I know, I—"

"It's okay. I love your mom. I won't say a word against her. But she has these strange ideas, you know? She thinks all sorts of things. Never mind. Not your fault. Nobody's fault. How are you? You doing great?"

"Uh, I guess."

"*I guess?* 'I guess' doesn't sound great."

"It's not. Things are, well…" My voice wobbles. "You know."

199

"Sure," he says gently. "I know. Sometimes life sucks, huh?"

"Yeah."

"So is that why you're calling? Something's wrong?"

"Maybe." Do I tell him? This is so hard. "You'll think I'm nuts."

"Don't tell me what I'll think. I'd never think that."

"Everyone else does."

"Who cares about everyone else?"

Before I can stop myself I say, "I need you. I do. I have no one else to talk to."

"What do you mean? You have your mom."

"I don't. I don't have anyone."

"Buddy, Buddy." He's so concerned I want to break. "What is it, Buddy? Go ahead. Tell me."

"Okay…" Here goes nothing. "Do you believe in ghosts?"

"Sure, why not? I mean, look, I've never seen one, never talked to one, never even come close. But there are so many stories, stories from people way smarter than me, and they swear they've seen them, talked to them. All those stories… You know what they say, Buddy—where there's smoke, there's fire."

"Yeah, I know." For the first time in ages, I'm breathing. Really breathing. "I think so too."

Out of nowhere, Mom's running up the stairs. "Cameron?" I hear Ken on her heels. "Cameron?"

"It's Mom. Gotta go," I whisper. "I'll call tomorrow from school."

I hang up and slip the photo and phone under my pillow as Mom and Ken barge into my room.

I jump up. "Hello? There's this new invention. It's called privacy."

Mom's eyes are wild. "Cameron, who were you talking to? Was it that ghost?"

"No," I shout. "It wasn't 'that ghost.' It was his buddies. The whole frigging cemetery. We were having a party."

"Don't talk to me like that."

Ken puts his arm around her. "We were worried about you."

"Don't be. I'm fine."

"No, Cameron," Mom says, "you're *not* fine." She has this look like my head's going to spin off and hit the ceiling. Maybe it is.

"If you're so worried," I rage, "why don't you sleep up here with Ken? Then you can eavesdrop on me all you like. Plus it'll save Ken having to sneak down to your room in the middle of the night. You think I don't hear the stairs?"

Mom's eyes flicker. Ken looks away. They separate.

*Oh my God. It's true.*

"You owe Ken an apology," Mom says. "And me." She turns on her heel and goes back downstairs. Ken shoots me an embarrassed glance and follows her.

So…Mom's sleeping with Ken. Maybe I guessed, but now I know. And after my call, I know something else even *more* important.

I'm not crazy. Neither is Dad.

# 37

There are things you want to know and things you don't. Right now, my head is full of so many things I don't want to know that I can't stand it. I rock on the edge of my bed. Right away, like he knew I needed him, Jacky's here beside me.

"It's tough, huh?" he says. "I didn't want to know about Mother's friend either."

"I don't know what I want. It's weird. I mean, I like Ken."

"But he's not your father."

"No, he's not Dad. Jacky, what am I going to do about Dad?"

"Don't worry," he says. "It'll all work out." His voice is so solemn, like he's the wisest person in the world. We sit a bit, then Jacky says, "I know it's bothered you, me not being around. I've been hiding in my secret place. I didn't want to think about that day with Father and the dogs."

"It's okay," I say, not wanting to scare him off. "You don't have to tell me."

"No, I do," he says quietly. "It's been my secret since forever. Secrets are hard, especially secrets like that. They don't leave you alone. I try to hide, to make them go away, but they don't, they won't. Cameron, I need to tell someone. You're the only one I can trust. Can I?"

"Are you sure?"

"Please. Just look away is all. It's easier to say it if you look away."

"Okay." I stare at the spot by the window where the wallpaper's peeling back. Soon I see double, triple. Things blur and disappear, and all I'm aware of is the sound of Jacky's voice.

"After Mother left and the police came by, Father got rid of the telephone. It was ringing at weird times, and he thought I might answer. About a week later, he got the dogs. They came in steel cages. He fed them in the barn but let them run free. He said they were to keep people away, people who'd take me, who'd hurt me. But the dogs kept me inside too. I was scared to go out. I saw them from the window, chasing rabbits, and how the rabbits never knew where to run, like they'd forgotten how, and how the dogs ripped them apart.

"In my dreams I was a rabbit.

"Father knew I was scared. He said it was good, that it kept me in line. When I'd be bad or say I wanted to see Arty, he didn't put me in the coal room anymore. Instead he grabbed me and dragged me to the door. 'Go ahead,' he'd yell. 'Go see Arty. Get put in some orphanage with the rats. See if I care.' And I'd hear the dogs barking, and I'd hold on to anything, the counter, the door frame, anything to keep from being thrown outside. Anything to keep away from the dogs.

"I sort of knew he'd never feed me to them. I even liked it when he got mad and dragged me to the door. Because afterward he'd hold me and tell me he loved me."

Jacky stops talking. I hear his breath though, fast and hard, exactly in time with my own. I want to ask what happened that day. But I know it's hard when you get to the part you can't say, the part you don't want to remember, so I stay real still. I just stare at the wall and wait until he's ready to tell me the thing he's never told.

"It was a Sunday morning," Jacky says at last. "I know because we always listened to the church service on the radio. Father had been drinking. After Mother went away, he drank all the time. He was looking gray and getting nightmares, yelling Mother's name and the name of her friend, and how it wasn't his fault, it was *their* fault things happened.

"Anyway, it was right in the middle of the sermon. We were in the kitchen, and Father was pacing back and forth talking to himself. All of a sudden he seized up, grabbed his arm, and went stiff. Then he toppled over, hit his head on the floor, and lay there.

"At first I thought he'd just knocked himself out. So I shook him. 'Father? Father?' Nothing. I turned him over. He stared up at me. I slapped his face. 'Wake up, wake up.' He didn't, just kept staring. I told myself everything was okay. But it wasn't. I knew it. He was dead.

"I didn't know what to do. I couldn't call out; there was no phone. And I couldn't go over to Arty's because of the dogs. They were barking, scratching at the door. He hadn't fed them. I knew they must be hungry, so I got some hamburger, chicken, and a few vegetables out of the fridge. I tossed them at the dogs from my bedroom window. They went crazy, fighting for everything.

"At night I stayed beside Father so I wouldn't be lonely, because there was nobody but me and him, and the dogs outside. I needed

Father. He always knew what to do. Only now he was all stiff and staring at me. I tried to close his eyelids. They wouldn't. So I wrapped his head in a towel, covered him in a blanket, and snuggled under to be near him.

"I stayed with Father for three days, throwing all the food I could find at the dogs. It was never enough. Then Father started to smell, the kind of smell that got on the frying pan when he didn't wash it. It got so bad I couldn't take it. I rolled him to the door to put him in the fresh air. I waited till I didn't hear the dogs. Then I opened it.

"But some of them were just outside. They leaped at Father's body. I raced upstairs. They followed me. I climbed the ladder into the attic and pulled up the ladder. There were dogs everywhere now, all over the house. I closed the trapdoor so I couldn't see them. But I could still hear them, ripping at Father, tearing at him. It was my fault. All my fault. I screamed and screamed and ran to Mother's hope chest. I crawled inside, closed the lid, stuck my fingers in my ears, and sang songs so I wouldn't hear. At last I fell asleep."

Oh no. I understand now. "What happened when you woke up?" I whisper. But I know the answer.

"It was dark," he sniffles. "I just stayed there."

"In your mother's hope chest. Your secret hiding place?"

"Yeah."

Where is it now? I wonder. But all I say is, "You did good."

"No."

"I mean it. You were braver than I'll ever be. Even now. I couldn't be alone all these years like you."

"I haven't always been alone. Arty moved here for a while. Only he looked older. He wouldn't talk to me. He didn't want to play anymore. Then you came." His voice goes shy. "I'm glad you're my friend."

"So am I."

"And the dogs. They've been here too. Like I told you. They're everywhere. They see everything."

I seize up.

"No, it's okay. Don't be scared. They won't hurt you. I won't let them."

"But what they did to your father…"

"That was my fault. They were hungry. But they're not anymore. When I went to sleep I dreamed we were playing. We've been playing ever since."

"All the same, when I hear them howling in the wind…the way they howl…"

"That's just how they sound. Things aren't always what you think. We imagine all kinds of stuff that isn't true. You know that, right?"

I nod.

"Father said he got the dogs to keep me safe. To protect me from bad people who'd take me away. They did too. And they'll protect you, if you want." I feel him give me a hug, like a little brother. "I have to go now."

And he's gone.

# 38

Everyone's pretty quiet at breakfast. Ken smiles for a living, so a couple of times he tries to loosen things up by wondering if it'll snow or starting a funny story, but Mom says, "Ken, not now," and he shuts up.

If things were weird at breakfast, they're even weirder when Mom drives me to school. Tomorrow's the weekend. Even classes would be better than two days of this.

Mom finally breaks the silence. "Do you have something to say to me?"

"Like what?"

"I have to spell it out?"

"Oh, like, sorry for what I said about you and Ken?"

"Something like that."

"Why should I be sorry? It was the truth. Do you have something to say to *me*?"

Mom shoots me a look. "Such as?"

"Did you go out with other guys before Ken?"

"That's none of your business."

"So you did."

Mom takes a deep, angry breath. "If you must know, on occasion I was asked out for dinner. The last time was a year ago."

"Why didn't you tell me?"

"I wanted to wait till I was sure I'd found the right person."

I stare out the window. "Did you ever 'go out for dinner' when we were with Dad?"

"Cameron!"

"Did you? Is that why he got mad?"

"Of course not. I suppose you heard him yelling things. He had a wild imagination. He made up stories that weren't true."

"In other words, he was like me."

"That's not what I said."

"Would you tell me if his stories were true?"

Mom clenches the steering wheel. "This conversation is over." We stay silent the rest of the way to school.

I get out of the car. "Thanks."

Mom drives off without a word. The silent treatment is her way to punish me. Well, it doesn't work. I have Dad to talk to. He's all I think about till lunch. I don't even care when Cody's friend, Brandon, jabs me with a pen and says, "Watch your back, dickhead. We haven't forgotten. We know where you live."

At guidance, I wave to Ms. Adams as I go into her conference room. Then I get out my sandwich, phone, and calling card and dial.

"Hey, Buddy. Long time, no talk to," Dad says, laughing.

"Last night Mom thought I was talking to a ghost." I laugh back.

"Guess I *have* been a kind of a ghost since she took you away. There in spirit, even if you couldn't see me."

"Yeah." I hesitate. "Dad, I hate to ask, but have you been trying to find us? Like, have you been after us?"

"Is that what your mom says?"

"It's not just her. There was that Facebook thing."

"I'm sorry about that," Dad says quietly. "It's just—Cameron, I love you. What kind of father wouldn't look for his son?"

"I don't know."

"Well, I don't know either. You're the most precious thing in the world to me, Buddy. Every night I dream about you, wonder about you, worry about you. I wouldn't be a father if I didn't."

"Yeah."

"I'll bet she's called me a stalker. Reported me to the police." I don't say anything; he reads my mind. "I thought so. Your grandparents— well, I'm not going to talk about them. I'm sure they love you very much. But they, well… I'm sorry, there are things I shouldn't say."

"No, say it."

"I wish I could. But parents shouldn't say things about each other, or about grandparents either. It isn't fair. You wouldn't make up things about someone who wasn't around to defend himself, would you?"

"No."

"Good boy. When a parent or grandparent lies about the other parent, it can mess a kid up." He pauses. "Anyway, it's true that I hired a private investigator. I don't know everything he did. All I know is, he cost me a lot of money. But you were worth it. Things weren't the same without you."

My heart beats a little faster. "So, like, you know where we've lived?"

"Not really. He wasn't very good. I think you maybe moved twice?"

"Four times."

"Four? That's a lot."

"Yeah. Mom kept saying she could tell when you were around. She said she could feel it. That you were around where she worked or parked outside at night, all kinds of stuff."

"The mind can sure play tricks, can't it? I guess you figured out that if what she said was true, I'd have been arrested."

"I kind of thought so, yeah."

"And I wasn't, was I?" He sighs. "It must have been hell, moving all those times. Leaving friends. Thinking this psycho dad was out to get you."

"It was pretty awful."

"I hear you, Buddy. Just remember, my name is Mike."

"Huh?"

Dad chuckles. "Mike. It's a good, solid name, like Cameron. A name you can trust. Not a name like Cody."

"What?" My throat goes dry.

"Or Jason. Or Colt. Or Zach. You know, cool names, tough-guy names."

I can't breathe. "Why did you say Cody?"

"What do you mean? You know a Cody?"

"Maybe."

"You like him?"

"No."

"So what did I tell you?" Dad laughs again. "For a second I thought you were going paranoid like your mom."

"Dad, I gotta go," I lie. "The bell's going to ring."

"Bye for now then," Dad says. "Talk to you later."

"You bet."

I hang up. *Cody? What was that all about?*

# 39

The Cody thing freaks me all day. It's like my brain is jammed. In the middle of the night I wake up, wild-eyed and sweating: what have I done?

*Nothing. Called Dad. Big deal.*

Something's wrong. Dad knows about Cody.

*It was a fluke. He said his name along with a bunch of others.*

No, I gave away where we are.

*How?*

I don't know, but I did. Dad's coming for us. It's my fault. I have to tell Mom.

*Are you kidding? She'll go nuts. And for nothing.*

But if Dad comes, he could hurt us. He could kill us—

*That's Mom talking. Remember Dad's voice. He sounded nice.*

Anyone can sound nice.

*Dad's not coming, because it's impossible for him to know where we are. He got called on a calling card. And besides, remember that first call? He said not to tell him where we were because Mom would get mad. That means he doesn't know and he doesn't want trouble.*

But what if he *does* know?

*What if ducks ride bicycles? Don't be an idiot. If Dad comes, Ken's here. Ken's a big guy. No way Dad could pull anything with Ken around. We'll be fine.*

But, but, but, but, but—

It's like that all night, me arguing with myself. I hold the pillow between my teeth to keep from talking out loud.

I get up early and brush my teeth. I can't believe I'm the guy in the mirror. My face is gray as a corpse, my eyes puffy as gym bags. Saturday. A weekend with Mom and Ken. *Can I please die now?*

They're already in the kitchen. They must hear me moving around, because they go quiet, like they've switched to whispers and hand signals. I go downstairs thinking about my secret calls and wondering what Mom and Ken were saying. I can't look them in the eye, not when I know I should tell about Dad but can't without setting off World War III.

"Rough night?" Mom's voice is gentle, which makes me feel even worse.

"Yeah." I slump into my chair

She brings me my cereal. "We didn't sleep very well either."

"I'm sorry," I say quietly. "Really sorry."

Mom squeezes my shoulders, happy and surprised. I'm pretty sure she thinks I'm talking about what I said about her and Ken. If that gets me out of talking about calling Dad, great. She motions to Ken and they sit opposite me. "We're sorry too. Ken, do you want to start?"

"Sure." Ken leans over the table, trying to make eye contact. I glance at him. "You and I, we went off the rails a few weeks ago. It was my fault. You trusted me with something and I told your mom. I should've been clear I'd be telling her and explained why. We could have talked about it, maybe spoken to your mom together. But I went ahead and you got ambushed. That wasn't fair, and it's on me. I apologize."

I look up slowly. Ken's giving me the puppy eyes he had when we talked about his kids.

"Yeah, well, okay," I say slowly. "I mean, I kind of know why you thought you had to tell. And, yeah, if you'd told me first, I probably wouldn't have been so mad. Anyway, thanks."

"So we're good?"

"I guess. Sure."

"I have something I'm sorry about too," Mom says, and takes my hand. "I should have talked to you about bringing Ken into our life as more than a friend. Sneaking around is a terrible thing, no matter how old you are. We've been talking—if you'd rather he stays at his own place, he will."

"Absolutely," Ken says. "This is your home. I'm just a guest."

"Sort of more than a guest." I manage a smile.

"Anyway…" Mom lets the choice dangle.

I stare at my cereal. I know Mom's never getting back with Dad and she deserves to be with someone. Ken doesn't get in my face or try to boss me around, and I know he cares about us. Plus if Dad ever shows up and tries something—I mean, he won't, but if he does—then Ken can take care of it and I won't have to feel like I put Mom in danger.

Ken clears his throat. "Maybe I should go upstairs so you and your mom can talk about this privately."

"No, it's okay." I look up. "You can stay if you want. Only—I know this sounds weird, but I just don't want to hear anything, if you know what I mean."

Mom blushes. "Of course."

"Not that I *have*. I mean, I haven't."

Mom and Ken look relieved. Mom squeezes my hand. Ken reaches across the table and holds my other one, then they take each other's.

"From now on, no more secrets," Mom says. "Agreed?"

Ken and I nod. "Agreed."

As if that's even possible.

# 40

**N**ormally conversations like that make me embarrassed. Not today. Instead my worry bubble pops, and out of nowhere I'm flying. I feel safe: Mom and Ken are on my side. Why did I ever think Dad could make trouble? In fact, I feel so good I wash the dishes without being asked and make my bed so the blankets don't hang below the bedspread, which according to Mom is a big deal.

Mom and Ken are suddenly different too. Mom looks younger, and Ken's back to being relaxed. It's like we live in Happyville. In the late morning, Ken takes us over to Ramsay, where there's an actual French bistro. Mom and Ken have fancy-sounding pasta with squid and mussels and a salad of avocado and red leaves. I have a cheeseburger and fries—correction, a *hamburger aux trois fromages et pommes frites*.

Still, like always, as soon as one worry cartwheels out of my brain circus, another one somersaults into the ring. This new worry starts on the road back home. What do I do about Dad? I mean, it's great knowing he's still around and cares about me, but I can hardly keep doing our secret calls.

*Why not?*

I can't take the lying. Too much stress.

*There's a difference between keeping a secret and lying.*

It doesn't feel like it. Mom won't think so either. Sooner or later she'll find out or I'll say something to Dad that *will* give us away.

*If you stop calling, Dad'll be upset.*

I know. So what do I tell him?

We get back home late afternoon. I go upstairs to do some homework while Mom and Ken have a nap. That's what they're calling it anyway. I put on my headphones, turn up the volume, and try to do math. The numbers float in front of my eyes.

I look out at the barn. If I'm right, two bodies are buried in there. I imagine Mr. McTavish digging the graves and Mrs. McTavish's face, dead, eyes wide open in horror. I think of Mom's face. What would she look like dead? And Ken. And me. *Stop. This is sick.*

I grip the sides of my desk and count to ten. It doesn't work. Something else suddenly scares me. Someone or something is in the barn watching me.

*Right. Like when I pictured mutants behind the furnace, dogs in the cornfield, and bodies taped up in the attic.*

No. This is real.

*The corn's down. No one could get to the barn without being seen.*

They could've arrived last night or when we were at lunch.

*But who?*

Mr. Sinclair?

*He's weird, but he's not a perv.*

Dad?

*He doesn't know where we live.*

220

Cody knows. "Watch your back, dickhead. We haven't forgotten. We know where you live." That's what his buddy Brandon said.

*Why would Cody do something here?*

To prove he can get me anywhere.

*He wouldn't risk it. After your fight, he'd be the main suspect.*

Not if he sent his gang and had an alibi. They can wait for me to step outside or break in at night. If they're in disguise, how can I prove anything?

*Come on, it's just your imagination.*

Is it?

I'm nervous all through dinner, but I don't say anything. If I tell Mom and Ken, they'll think I'm hallucinating again, and everything will be wrecked, just when they're starting to act like I'm normal again. I shove a few peas around with my fork.

"What the matter?" Mom asks.

Uh-oh. "Was I talking out loud?"

"No. But you've got worry written all over your face. And you've hardly said a word since coming to the table."

I try to fake a smile. "It's only math. There's a couple of formulas I don't get."

"Want us to have a look after the dishes?" Ken asks. "Between your mom and me, we might be able figure it out with you."

"Sure," I say. Having them around will keep me distracted.

It did too. But soon it's lights out. I lie in bed all night imagining the worst. Every sound is huge—the coyotes in the distance, the dogs in the wind.

At Sunday breakfast Mom and Ken catch me moving my lips.

"Cameron, talk to us," Mom says. "You're thinking about more than a few math problems."

"It's nothing."

"If it was nothing, you wouldn't be like this."

I put down my spoon and look from Mom to Ken and back again. "I'm imagining something, okay? So no big deal. It's not real. It's all in my head."

"That's an important thing to know," Mom says. "A major first step."

Ken frowns. "But it doesn't get rid of the fear, does it? Maybe if we knew where it's coming from, we could do something to fix it."

*Nice. As long as I say what I'm thinking's not real, they'll take it seriously.*

"Mom"—how do I put this?—"remember how sometimes you'd think Dad was in a car in the shadows across the street?"

"He was."

"Right. But you never actually saw him."

"I didn't need to. I knew."

"Okay, well, it's like that when I look at the barn. I haven't seen anyone, but I think someone's watching me."

Mom tenses. "Your father?"

"I don't know who. Cody maybe? Or some of his gang?"

"But this is all in your head, correct?"

"I guess. I don't know."

"It's hard to live without fear after all your father did," Mom says. "But you're safe now."

"All the same, this Cody kid *is* in the area," Ken says. "We know he wouldn't *really* come on the property. But it doesn't stop the worry, does it?" He gives me a reassuring smile. "Why don't we check out the barn after breakfast to clear your mind? It's always best to face our fears."

"I know, and I do that all the time with pretend stuff, like checking out zombies in the furnace room. But..." My voice trails off.

"I can go by myself, if you'd like," Ken says.

"No, I don't want you getting hurt."

"Why would Ken get hurt?" Mom asks. "There's nothing there. I say we should all go out. I've never been inside that barn. It'd be interesting."

"No. Look, I'll go with Ken. You stay inside in case there's a problem. I mean, there won't be, but just in case. I'll have my phone."

Mom and Ken exchange glances. "Fine," Mom says. "I expect a full report and then we can all have a good laugh."

Ken and I walk back to the barn. I try not to glance up at the hole in the loft. We go inside and turn on our flashlights. We scan the ground floor; shadows roam from stall to stall.

"Let's start at opposite sides and go up and down the aisles till we meet in the middle," Ken says. "That way our imaginary intruder won't be able to escape. If you see anything, yell. I'll be right over."

What a baby I am. With Ken here, last night feels like a dream, especially with him whistling pop songs. The shadows are creepy, sure, but that's normal. I mean, it's an old barn...and it has dead bodies in it. Where are Mrs. McTavish and Matthew Fraser buried? I imagine their bones poking through the ground in the stall ahead of me, and the one after that, and the one after that, till Ken and I finally meet up.

"See anything?" he asks.

"No."

"Good. Let's check the loft and get back inside. It's cold." He grins. "Your mom's sure right about needing to dress warm."

We start climbing the stairs, Ken first, me looking back over my shoulder even though I know no one's behind me. *Please let the upstairs be empty. Please let there be nobody there either.*

We get to the top. What a relief. There's nothing here but the birds on the rafters.

"Feel better?" Ken asks.

I nod. "Sorry for all the…you know."

"No big deal. Being scared is nothing to be ashamed of. We all are from time to time." He laughs. "Someday I'll have to tell you how scared I was of you the first time we really talked, that morning you came to my office."

"You were scared of *me*?"

"No kidding. I thought, If this kid hates me, I'm toast with Katherine."

I smile. "Yeah, well, I'm a scary guy. Ask anyone."

Ken gives me a pat. "Okay, inside. I want a coffee." He heads below.

What an idiot I was. I shake my head and go to leave. At the top of the stairs I have one last look around.

A cold, sick feeling fills my stomach. When I was here before, an old pail was on its side in the middle of the room. It's not there anymore. It's beside the hole in the wall, turned upside down to make a stool. Cody probably used it while he watched me in my room.

I have to tell Ken. No, hold on. What if *I* used it when I spied on Mr. Sinclair? That was so far back, I can't remember. I could have moved it without thinking, probably did. One thing's for sure though. From now on, I'm keeping my curtains closed. And I'm not going outside alone.

# 41

Monday morning, Mom drives me to school. I'm totally messed up about Cody spying on me, but mainly about how to break the news to Dad that we can't talk anymore. I don't want to hurt his feelings, what with him so excited, but sneaking around on Mom isn't right. How do I let him down gently?

At lunchtime, I take my phone and calling card into the guidance conference room and dial his number.

Two rings and he picks up. "Buddy?"

"Yeah."

"I've practically sat on this phone since Friday. If it was an egg, it would've hatched."

I try to laugh, but it sticks in my throat.

"What's up, Buddy?"

"Well…Dad…there's a couple of things on my mind…"

"Such as?"

"Such as…Dad, you know I've missed you, right?"

"Right. I've missed you too."

"And it's really meant a lot to talk to you. You've been great. And I wish we could talk more. We will…"

Dad's voice clouds over. "I hear a pretty big 'but' coming up."

"Yeah. See, the thing is, right now isn't such a great time for us to be talking."

"Says who?"

"Me, I guess. We need to take a break."

Silence.

"Dad? Dad, are you there?"

"I'm here," he says quietly.

"Good. Anyway, Dad, I want you to know it's nothing you've done. It's me. I feel weird going behind Mom's back."

"So your mother's the reason. I knew it. Don't let her push you around, Buddy. She does that. She makes people do things they regret."

"No. It's not Mom. The sneaking just makes me feel creepy. In a few years, when I'm on my own, calling again would be great. Seeing you would be even better."

"But for now," Dad says, all cold, "it's just toss your dad off a cliff. Is that what I'm hearing? Because that's what it sounds like. You want to kick me into the ditch because you don't have the balls to stand up for yourself. To say, 'Mom, I have a dad. I want to see him.'"

"No! It's not like that!"

"Sure it is, Buddy. She has you wrapped around her little finger."

"She doesn't. There's other things, lots of other things. I'm really confused right now. I need space."

"Space from your dad? I'm your friend, Buddy. You have a problem, you tell me and I'll help."

"You can't. Remember that Cody guy at my school?"

"What did he do this time?"

"Him and his gang—I think they're spying on me. I'm not positive, but it sure feels like it."

"That's serious," Dad says slowly. "Do you have a dog? Maybe a dog pack?"

"A dog pack?" My stomach churns.

"They'd bark if there were strangers around."

"Why are you talking about dog packs?"

"Settle down, Buddy. It was advice, that's all. You know how your mother talks about me? I'm actually surprised she doesn't have a pack of dogs to keep me away."

I start to sweat. Dad knows things. I don't know how, but he does. I have to do something. "Actually, Mom *did* get us a dog," I lie. "A guard dog. He's vicious with strangers. Like, if anybody came around, he'd tear them apart."

"Oh?" Dad sounds amused. "What's his name?"

"Rex. He's a Rottweiler."

"You sure about that?"

"Of course I'm sure. He's my dog."

"They let dogs in your building?"

"Yes." My heart races. "Up to two. Mom says we should maybe get another to keep him company."

"So you live in a building, not a house."

"Y-yes," I stammer.

"Strange your dog doesn't bark when Cody's around. Sounds like a useless guard dog."

"We trained him to be quiet. We also have neighbors who watch out for us."

Dad chuckles.

"What's so funny?"

"You are. You sound so serious."

"I *am* serious. Anyway, like I said, I can't call anymore."

"You mean, you *won't*," Dad says.

"Right. Look, I have to go."

"Well, Buddy, you have to do what you have to do. So do I."

"What do you mean?"

"What I said." His voice is low. "I don't have much to live for without my Buddy."

Oh no, is he going to kill himself? "Dad, don't be like that. I said I'd call when I'm older."

"Right."

"Dad, promise you won't do something stupid."

"We all do stupid things, Buddy, things that can't be fixed. Things like running away and breaking up a family. Things like lying to the people who love us."

"Dad—"

"Say good-bye, son. Don't worry. We'll talk again. I'm just a phone call away."

The line goes dead.

# 42

I leave guidance without eating lunch. The halls are packed with people heading to afternoon classes. I stop for a drink at the fountain. When I straighten up, I practically walk into Cody.

"Boo."

I jump back.

"You spooked, Dog Boy? Only brave when you're stalking old women."

I look him in the eye. "I know what you're doing, Cody."

"What's that?" Cody smirks.

"Hiding in the barn. Spying on me."

"Have you gone wacko?"

"Stay off our property. I'm warning you. We're getting dogs. Guard dogs."

"Like that crazy farmer?" Cody taunts. "Oooh, I am, like, so scared."

"Screw you."

Cody's eyes narrow. "What did you say?"

"Boys?" It's Ms. Adams. "Get going. You'll be late for class."

Cody gives me the finger and slouches away. I take off in the opposite direction.

Somehow I make it to the end of the day without throwing up.

I wait for Mom in the office. Why are office benches so hard? To make kids uncomfortable before they see the VP? I don't care so much these days. The weather's been so cold I've been wearing my winter coat.

"Cameron, five o'clock," the head secretary says. "We're closing up. Can you let your mother know?"

"Sure."

I text her: School closed. Come get me?

She texts back: Right away.

The custodian lets me stand in the foyer till he goes to the back of the school to wash the gym floor, then he locks me outside. After all, can't leave a loony alone in the halls.

The sun's down, and it's starting to snow. The parking lot's empty, except for the custodian's Corolla. I think about Cody. His gang. *Where's Mom?*

The wind whips up. The snow stings my cheeks. Enough of this crap.

I send Mom another text: I'm outside freezing. Where are you?

She gets back right away: Sorry. Held up. Ken's on his way.

The next five minutes feels like forever. At last I see Ken's car. Whew. He stops at the side of the road. I jog out. He rolls down his window. Only it's not Ken.

"Hi, Buddy."

"Dad."

# 43

Dad smiles. "Hop in."

"Dad, what are you doing here?"

"Why, I've been at the motel next door since Saturday morning. Drove nonstop since our call on Friday. The room's not bad, but the coffee's crap."

I start to shake. "And Ken—what are you doing in Ken's car?"

"Ken? Don't I even get a 'Hi' first? You hurt my feelings."

"Okay, hi. So where's Ken?"

"Hop in and I'll tell you."

I think about running back to the school. For what? The doors are locked. Everyone's gone except the custodian, off in the gym.

Dad keeps smiling, but his voice is stone cold. "I said, 'Hop in,' Cameron."

I step back from the car, stick my hand in my pocket, and fumble for my phone.

I speed-dial Mom.

There's a ring in Dad's jacket pocket. He pulls out Mom's phone and talks into it. "Hello, Cameron? Is that you? I'm afraid your mom can't come to the phone right now. She's held up. Remember?"

I stand there frozen.

Dad flips the phone shut. "If you want to see your mother again, Buddy, give me your phone and get in the car."

My brain jams. I can't think. I hand Dad my phone and get in the car, like he's a zombie puppet master. *Is this real? Am I breathing?*

"That's my boy," Dad says, all friendly again. "You should unzip that coat. I've got the heat up."

I unzip my coat. "Mom." I can hardly get the words out. "Where's Mom? Ken?"

"Why do you care about Lover Boy?"

"Tell me."

"Fine," Dad sighs, disappointed. "Your mom's at the farmhouse. She's had a nasty tumble into the basement, but she's all right. You know the coal room? She's locked in there for her own good. You know how she likes to run. After a fall, that wouldn't be good."

Silence. Dad starts to drive. He's heading to the farm. I feel sick.

Dad sings, "I had a dog, his name was Rover." Only Dad sings "Rex." "You lied to me, Buddy. About the dog, the apartment building. You think I can't tell when you're lying? When your mother was lying?"

"Ken," I blurt out. "Where's Ken? What did you do to him? Why won't you say?"

Dad grips the wheel like he used to squeeze my arm. "As a matter of fact, Lover Boy is in the trunk," he says, super controlled. "Don't you remember anything? I texted: Ken's on his way. And he was. I've never lied to you. You and your mom, you've lied to me, but I've never lied to you."

Dad turns on the windshield wipers to brush back the snow.

"How did you find us?"

"There are lots of ways to find people, Buddy. No one can hide forever, not if someone wants to find them hard enough. You and your mom, you've been my hobby. You're all I've thought about. Your mom, she took everything from me. I lost my job, my savings, you. Finding you is all that's kept me going."

"But how did you find us this time?"

"Well, that's an interesting story." He settles back into his car seat. "I've had a Google alert on your name from the beginning. Every so often I thought I was wasting my time. Do you have any idea how many Cameron Weavers there are? How many have wedding and birth announcements, obituaries, and awards that get mentioned in local papers? No wonder your mom never changed your name. But I kept at it. Like I said, I've had time. And a couple of weeks ago it paid off."

"Huh? I wasn't in the papers."

"Maybe not, but you sure ticked off some kids at your school. Imagine my surprise when my Google alert spits out your name at this new blog: "Cameron Weaver Is a Dickhead." It's got photos too, and a comment section. This Cody Murphy, did you really stalk his great-granny? Like father, like son, huh?" He chuckles. "Someone said you deserved to be ripped apart by dogs, like the guy who used to live at your place. Kids can be cruel, huh?"

Oh my God. If I hadn't gone to the nursing home, none of this would be happening. *Mom, Ken, I'm sorry.*

"I don't get the feeling this Cody kid is all that bright, but I guess it doesn't take much to put up a blog these days. Just energy or hate. Me, I have energy; I never hate. But your mom—not a word against her, but hate's her middle name." He reaches over to Ken's iPod dock. "Want some music?"

"No," I whisper.

"Suit yourself." Dad turns up the windshield wipers. "You know, at first I wasn't sure that Cameron Weaver the Dickhead was you. I thought I might be heading off on a wild-goose chase, almost didn't come. I mean, this place is the farside of nowhere. But then you phoned. It was like a sign from God. I took a chance and mentioned the name Cody. The way you reacted, well, I knew I'd hit the jackpot."

*My fault. This is all my fault.* I can't see for all the snow in the headlights. Or is it my eyes filling? "How did you get Mom and Ken? You would've had to fight."

"Buddy, I never fight. I defend myself—that's different." He pauses. "To answer your question, I watched your mom drop you off this morning from the motel parking lot. I followed her to that real estate office, saw Lover Boy going in and out. I googled the office, sent him an email, said I was new in town, staying at the motel, and could he show me some properties. Sure enough, he picked me up. I got in the car and, well, he didn't say much when I showed him my gun."

*A gun. Dad has a gun.*

"I had Lover Boy drive to a country lane," Dad continues, "then I hog-tied him in the trunk. He kicked around a bit, but a whack to the head knocked some sense into him. Back in town, I parked by the rear door to the office. There was no one inside but your mom.

When I said I had you, she did what I wanted, meek as a lamb. So sweet. Reminded me of when we met."

"You said you had me? So you *do* lie."

"Buddy, why so harsh? I didn't have you then, but I have you now, don't I? I was just off by an hour."

I see our farmhouse in the distance.

"You were in the barn, weren't you? Why didn't you get us Saturday night?"

"I'm not stupid, Buddy. You're on one floor, your mom and Lover Boy are on another; you all have phones. Come on, give me some credit."

"So what are you going to do now?"

"Your mom's always made me do things I don't want to do. She'll never come back to me. And she won't let me have you. It isn't fair, is it? So what can I do? I don't have a choice."

I'm too scared to shake. "You're going to kill us?"

"A family needs to be together, Buddy. Lover Boy needs to pay. Once he pays, it'll be just the three of us."

Our farm's getting closer. I see the entrance to our lane.

Dad gets this sick smile. "Your mom will be crying, begging, no question. She's always tried to make me feel bad. Always tried to shift the blame."

"Leave Mom alone. I won't see you hurt Mom."

"Don't worry. I don't think a boy should see his mom die either. It isn't right. So instead I'll have you stand in front of her, and after you've said your good-byes, I'll make her watch what she's done. Then your mom and I will have a final talk. It may be painful—she always made it painful—but once it's over we'll be together forever."

# 44

Dad turns up our lane. He puts his foot on the accelerator, as if he can't wait.

"Dad, you can't do this."

"Who's to stop me?"

"*Me!*"

I throw myself across him, grab the wheel, and jerk it hard. The car flies off the lane into the field. "Mr. Sinclair!" No way he can hear me. I push on the horn with one hand and keep it down.

Dad struggles for control. "Settle down, Buddy."

I scrunch my knees and pull myself over the gear stick to his side. Dad punches me on the ear. I see stars. It doesn't matter. I keep hold of the wheel, horn blaring.

The car veers toward the woods. Dad tries to brake, but I jam a foot on the accelerator. Everything's a rush of snow, wipers, horn, headlights, shouting.

Suddenly, right ahead—the bushes in front of the woods. We're going to crash. I hurl myself toward the passenger side.

The car hits the bushes. We fly forward. I bang my shoulder by the glove compartment. Dad hits his head on the windshield. He falls back, bleeding.

I throw my door open. Dad grabs the back of my coat. He pulls me back, but my jacket's unzipped, and my arms slip through the sleeves. I scramble away as fast as I can into the bushes.

"Stop!" Dad yells. "Don't make this hard, Buddy."

I look back. Dad's out of the car. I'm alone. There's no one to help me.

"Jacky!" I shout. "Jacky!"

*I'm here, Cameron.*

"Dad's going to kill me."

*No. Remember the clearing? Get to the clearing.*

I make it past the bushes, into the woods. I stumble across dead branches. The snow's in my face. *Where am I?*

"Buddy, I see your tracks," Dad singsongs. His voice goes in and out of the wind.

What do I do? Where do I go?

*Don't give up, Cameron.*

I shield my eyes. In front of me I see fallen trees under a thin layer of snow. I recognize the one with the roots pointing to the sky. The clearing's ahead.

"You can run but you can't hide." Dad's voice is louder. Closer. "I've found you before. I'll find you now."

I'm dead. I'm dead.

*Keep going.*

I push on, make the clearing. "What now?"

*The boulders. Arty and me, we played in the boulders.*

I head toward them.

*Faster. Faster.*

A few more feet, I'm there. I crouch behind them, look back to the woods. All I see is snow. My eyes fill with tears and flakes. I search for a crawl space.

*To the right. There's an opening between the rocks.*

Here, yes. I pull myself inside as far as I can. All I hear is the wind and my heartbeat. Out of nowhere, everything goes still. There's just a breeze, a whistling through the rocks.

Where's Dad? Did my tracks fill in? Did I lose him in the snow? Maybe he passed through. Maybe he's gone. Yes, that's it. I picture him wandering in the woods, lost. Or on the run. He'll want to get out of here. He knows I'll be getting someone to call the police. Maybe he thinks they're already coming.

The storm picks up again. For the first time I realize how cold I am, and how my leg and shoulder hurt. It doesn't matter. I'm safe. I close my eyes. My fingers and toes stop tingling. I fill with a strange warmth. I start to drift.

*Cameron, no. You can't let up. It's dark. It's snowing. You'll freeze out here. And your mother and Ken, they're still locked up. Your father could kill them before he runs. You have to stop him.*

Mom. Ken. I give my head a shake. I have to save them. I go to crawl out of my hiding place. That's when Dad grabs my legs.

"Come out, come out, wherever you are."

I'm afraid to look back. I don't have to. I picture Dad on all fours outside the opening. There's a gash on his forehead from where he hit the windshield. His face is covered in blood and snow. It runs down his neck.

"You always loved that story." Dad pulls on my legs.

I brace myself tight with my elbows. The wind blows louder. Snow whips around the boulders.

"I said, 'Come out,' Buddy. You can't win. It's over. I'm stronger than you. I have a gun."

"Then shoot me! Go ahead! Let the neighbors hear! Let them call the police! Let them catch you, you psycho whack job!"

Dad roars and yanks my legs so hard I feel my arms pulling out of their sockets. He yanks again. As my arms give way, I hear a high, piercing whistle. Is it Jacky? The wind? I don't know. All I know is that the whistling turns into howling. It's so loud I can't hear myself think.

I feel Dad pulling me out. I close my eyes and wait for the end. Only the wind—it's not the wind. It's the dogs.

I see them bounding through the woods. Their heads are down. Their fur bristles. Their eyes burn like coals.

Dad hears them too. He's still on all fours. He turns his head. He sees the dogs racing toward him, ears back, teeth bared.

Dad lets go of my legs. He freezes in terror. The dogs leap in the air.

Dad screams.

# 45

I'm sitting on the living room couch between Mom and Ken. Mr. Sinclair is here too, along with police and paramedics. There are three police cars and an ambulance outside.

Mr. Sinclair was the one who called the cops. He heard the horn, looked out his window, and saw headlights, the car out of control, and the crash. He took his shotgun and a heavy-duty flashlight and went to see what was up. When he realized the car was empty, he headed into the woods. He heard some yelling and found me at the boulders.

Dad was already dead.

*Dad's dead.* I say it over and over. I can't believe it. *Dad's dead.*

I told Mr. Sinclair about Mom and Ken. We went to the car. The key was still in the ignition. We'd just gotten Ken out of the trunk when the first cops drove up with their flashers.

The cops called in reinforcements and brought us back to the house. Before they could tell me to stay put, I raced downstairs and got Mom out of the coal room. She and Ken hugged me tight and didn't let go till just now when the paramedics arrived.

The medics check us out. Mom has a sprained ankle, Ken's face is messed up, and I have a bruise on my shoulder. "Other than that, you seem be okay," one of them says. "To be on the safe side, we'd like to bring you to the hospital to be sure. They may want to keep you overnight. You're likely in shock."

"Fine," Mom says, "but not till you've finished what you have to do out there with the police." She means in the woods with Dad. She won't feel safe till she knows he's in a body bag. Neither will I.

The cops leave with the medics, except for the two who came by that night after the nursing home. The heavy one asks each of us to tell him what happened; the thin one sits on the piano bench and takes notes. We tell them, then wait, numb, till the others return. I hear the shed door open and the sounds of them stomping the snow off their boots.

*Dad's dead. Dad's dead.* Why don't I feel anything?

Our cop friends go out for a briefing, then they all come back into the room.

"So it's true?" Mom asks.

The heavy cop nods. "It seems his throat was ripped open by an animal. All we can think is a coyote. It's next to unheard of. But if he was down on all fours, bleeding in the dark, he'd have looked and smelled like wounded prey. One good bite to the jugular, and he'd have been gone in no time."

His partner nods. "Whatever it was, there aren't any tracks. The snow's seen to that. We'll have a sniffer dog sent over from Hamilton County, but with all the critters out here and in the ravines, who knows if we'll find the one that did it."

I want to tell them it wasn't a coyote, it was the dogs, but I'm not stupid.

"You're lucky to be alive," the heavy cop says.

There's a moment of silence. Mr. Sinclair's been sitting in the leather armchair in the corner, head bowed. "May I say something?" he whispers with a glance to Mom. "Something personal?"

"Certainly."

Mr. Sinclair shifts awkwardly in his seat. I've never seen him look so old. There's something in his voice and eyes that's different too.

"Would you like this just for the family?" the heavy cop asks.

"No, stay," Mr. Sinclair says quietly. "What I have to say is mainly for Cameron, but I don't care who hears it." He looks into my eyes. "After what happened tonight—with you, with your mother, with your father…well…there's something I never thought I'd say, but it's something you deserve to know."

I'm half afraid to hear. "What?"

"The boy who lived here when I was your age, Jacky McTavish, he's been on your mind since the day we met."

I nod.

"His father was like yours. I saw the bruises. McTavish said Jacky got them from playing. But I was the one he played with, and he never got bruised around me." Mr. Sinclair closes his eyes; his forehead presses down. "The last time I saw Jacky alive, we were in the clearing. He was crying that his mother had run off with somebody, that she didn't want him, and from now on he'd have to stay inside. He made me promise not to tell. He said if I told, something terrible would happen to him. I knew what his father was like. So I promised I wouldn't tell.

"Later I heard my parents whispering that Jacky's mother had taken him away with Matthew Fraser. Father said, 'It's not proper,' but Mother said, 'Even if it isn't, it's a good thing. How Evelyn's managed to stay with Frank so long is a mystery known only to God.' I heard kids gossip at school. They said things about Jacky's mother, how she was a whore, and no wonder Jacky was so strange. But they didn't know Frank McTavish. And they didn't know what Jacky was like when he wasn't at school being picked on."

Mr. Sinclair sucks in his breath again and again. "I should have said something. I never did. I kept that stupid promise because I was afraid for Jacky and what would happen if I told. Then McTavish got the dogs, and within a month he was dead. When Jacky wasn't found there afterward, I figured his mother had come back and got him.

"My father was McTavish's executor. He paid the taxes on the farm and worked it. He said he was keeping it for when Mrs. McTavish or Jacky would come back to claim it. We thought they would too, in the beginning. By the time you wonder if maybe no one's ever coming back, things are the way they are, and life goes on. McTavish had no other kin. We had squatter's rights to the farm, so why think the worst, even if it's true? Better to imagine happy endings.

"I moved out of my parents' home and into here in my twenties. I moved everything on the first two floors into the basement. It was all junk by then, but in my head I was still saving it for Jacky, and I'm a hoarder at the best of times." Mr. Sinclair glances at me. "I don't believe in ghosts. Never have, never will. But I don't mind saying now that I had dreams about Jacky too. He wanted us to play, and I'd wake up thinking of our times in the clearing, and him and that damned fool cap I'd given him.

"When I was thirty-two there was a storm. Some shingles blew off, and I knew it was time to do the roof or there'd be more leaks than there already were. So for the first time I went up to the attic to check out the damage from the inside. At the end of the attic, there was a hope chest—his mother's, I figured. I opened it to see what was inside, expecting maybe some blankets. And there he was: Jacky, wearing the clothes he always wore and that Davy Crockett cap. Poor little tyke. I'm guessing he crawled inside to get away from the dogs and the lock fell shut and he couldn't get out.

"For the first few weeks after I found him, I didn't know what to do. I'd go up to the attic every night and stare at little Jacky in his hope chest. I knew if I didn't do something, I'd go crazy. One morning I made my decision. I brought him and the chest downstairs and sealed up the attic." Mr. Sinclair exhales. "It's my fault. If only I hadn't kept that stupid promise, if only I'd told the truth, that Jacky didn't go with his mother, that her letter was a lie, he might be alive today."

There's a long silence.

"What did you do with the body?" I ask quietly. "I mean, there wasn't a problem with you farming the land. You wouldn't have been in trouble, so why didn't you just report it?"

Mr. Sinclair wipes his eyes with the back of his sleeve. "I was afraid he'd end up buried in his family's plot. I knew since Evelyn's letter was wrong that McTavish had killed her. How could I see Jacky trapped forever with the monster who'd murdered his mother and made their lives a living hell?" He pauses. "Jacky had been dead over twenty years. No one was looking for him. Nobody cared. Well, I cared. I buried him in his mother's hope chest in the clearing by the boulders, the one place where he'd been happy."

My shoulders start to shake. Mom puts her arm around me.

"You may not have known everything you thought you knew," Mr. Sinclair tells me gently, "but you're a pretty good guesser."

"I suppose the only thing we'll never know is where Frank McTavish disposed of the bodies," says the thin cop.

"He buried them in the cow stalls," I say.

The cops share a here-we-go-again look. But I keep going, strong and clear: "Mr. McTavish knew he had to bury them. If their bodies or bones showed up, he'd be the first suspect. But it was March. The ground was still frozen. Only a backhoe could break it—and that would've drawn attention and made the graves obvious. The one place warm enough where he could dig in secret, where the bodies would never be found by accident, was the dirt floor inside his barn."

When the cops were here before, they wanted to scare me. Tonight, so far, they've tried to comfort me. Now, for the first time, they look at me with respect.

"That sure could be a possibility," the thin cop says, tapping his knee with his pen. "Brian, what do you say we get the team to investigate?"

# 46

Mom, Ken, and I get checked out at the hospital. We're all okay, but they keep us overnight for observation. When we get home, workers are already excavating the cow stalls, and others have a backhoe in the clearing. Mr. Sinclair is showing them where to dig. By late afternoon, they have the bodies and send them to the coroner for an official cause of death.

"What'll happen to Jacky now?" I ask Ken.

"We'll have to see," he says.

At dinner, Mom's in another world. She waits till we're ready to leave the table, then says calmly, "I've called your aunt Lorraine."

I've heard about Aunt Lorraine, but we've never met. She's Dad's younger sister, the last of his family. They stopped speaking to each other before I was born. Dad always said she was crazy, like he said about Mom.

"She's making arrangements for your father. He'll be prepared here and transported to a funeral home near her the day after tomorrow. There won't be a service. I don't want to upset you, but I need to ask… Did you want to see him before he goes?"

"I don't know."

"Think about it. Whatever you decide is fine."

We clear the dishes like Mom hasn't said anything. Then I go to my room and torture myself.

*I can't see him.*

I have to.

*Why?*

He was my dad.

My forehead tingles. It's like he's staring at me. I turn around and see the framed photograph of Mom and me and my grandparents on my bedside table, the one with the snapshot of him hidden underneath. I undo the frame, take out Dad's photo, and stare back at it.

In the picture, Dad and I are sitting cross-legged on the beach, where we've just made a sand castle. He has his arm around my shoulder; I'm holding up my plastic shovel like I'm a castle warrior. We look happy. Were we?

I look deep into Dad's eyes. What was he thinking? Who was he? I imagine him talking to me out of the picture. "Buddy, it's me, Dad. You have me all wrong."

I rip the picture to bits. My heart beats like crazy. It's the only picture of Dad I have. What if I want to see him again? I won't. I should flush the pieces down the toilet or burn them on the gas stove, but I'd feel too guilty. Instead I seal them in an envelope, take them to the basement, and lock them in the coal room. It's all I can think to do.

Next morning at breakfast, I tell Mom, "I don't want to see him." My face goes funny. I can hardly breathe. "I'm not like him. Please tell me I'm not like him."

"Cameron, you'll never be like that. You have feelings. You care about people."

I cry.

Mom says I can stay home from school until I feel ready to go back. She'll get homework from my teachers. Good. No way do I want people all around, asking me questions.

Grandma and Grandpa arrive in the middle of the morning. They drove all night. It's weird seeing them in person again. All the happy feelings I used to have when I'd see them come flooding back. Grandpa's whiskers still tickle when he rubs his chin on my forehead—which is kind of embarrassing now. Grandma still smells of apples and cinnamon.

They'll be here for a few days. Mom's put them in the big room down the hall from me; Ken's staying in her room. My grandparents like Ken a lot. He's been part of our last few calls. They tease him with the kind of jokes that old people think are funny.

For the next couple of days Grandma and Grandpa sit with me at a card table working on jigsaw puzzles. They brought a ton. I always thought jigsaws were stupid, but it's nice to be with them, thinking about nothing except separating the corner and outside pieces and figuring out what goes where.

Friday, Ken brings home this week's *Bugle*. The front-page headline is: "Local Boy Solves Murders." The story has my picture and the cops calling me "a brilliant young detective" and other stuff that makes Mom proud.

Just below, there's a write-up of how Dad wanted to kill us, and how I fought him off and he was killed in a coyote attack. "Sniffer dogs didn't turn up anything," their handler says. "They ran in circles like they were chasing ghosts." The head of animal control says that although coyote attacks are extremely rare, "for the time being joggers should stick to main trails."

Inside the paper, there's an article headlined: "Fifty Years Later, Hannah Murphy Vindicated." Cody and his family are pictured with his great-grandmother at the nursing home; he's holding her hand. Cody's grandfather says how much they all want to thank me for clearing her name and reputation. Once the coroner's work is finished, they'll be burying Matthew Fraser with his family.

The other news of the day comes from Mr. Sinclair.

"I've finally seen a lawyer about the farm," he tells us. "Seeing as my family tended it and paid the taxes for fifty years, he says there won't be a problem with the claim. I knew that. Still, it's a load off. There's nothing like having things certain."

By the end of the weekend, I'm getting restless and tell Mom I want to go back to school. It's strange going through the front door. It's not like I had friends before, but I'm happy to just see people.

As it turns out, they're happy to see me too. Everyone knows about the *Bugle* articles, not to mention that the story was on local TV and radio. All that, plus the public thank-you from Cody's family, get me back into class. In the cafeteria, kids I don't even know stare at me in awe. A few girls even hang around my locker. One of them asks for my autograph: "You're, like, a hero." As if. Still, apart from blushing, I feel pretty cool signing my name.

Benjie comes up to me. "I'm sorry I was mean to you."

"Don't be. I was the one who was mean. I lied and got you in trouble. Friends shouldn't do that."

"Friends?" Benjie blinks twice. "You mean we're friends?"

"Sure."

Benjie stinks and he's kind of irritating. All the same, he was nice to me when everybody else treated me like dirt. That counts for a lot. And if one of the girls who's hanging around my locker talks to him because he's a friend, well, I owe him. Also, it might get him to brush his teeth.

I know Cody's grateful about his great-grandmother, but he doesn't say much. I didn't expect him to. Still, he and his gang give me that tough-guy "You're okay" nod in the halls. To tell the truth, I'm glad he doesn't try to buddy up. Who needs a jerk in their life? It's enough to know I won't be getting spitballs anymore.

The other one who doesn't say anything is Jacky. Will I see him again? I don't know. He comes and goes when he wants. Now that his secrets are out, maybe he's happy to stay in the clearing with the dogs.

Secrets have such a weight. When they're off, you're lighter than air. Maybe that's it. Maybe Jacky's free in the air.

# 47

Today I meet Dr. Harrison, the psychiatrist in Ramsay. When I first got referred I didn't want to go, but now, even when I'm awake, I get flashes of Dad. Like, on our way to Dr. Harrison's office, we pass the bus station and I see the sign: "Elm Street." There's a guy getting out of his car. For a second I imagine it's Dad getting out of Matthew Fraser's Pontiac.

Dr. Harrison has a homey office in the Ramsay Medical Clinic. She's older than Mom, with a bony face and long fingernails. I thought I'd have to lie on a couch, but she points me to a leather armchair. She sits on the one opposite and picks up a pen and notepad from a side table.

"So, what would you like to talk about?" She smiles and waits for me to answer.

I shrug and sit there, hoping she'll say something else. She doesn't. Eventually the silence gets too weird so I say, "I guess you heard about what happened with my dad."

I know she must have, but she doesn't let on. "Would you like to tell me?"

"Not really."

More silence. I look at her desk lamp, the box of Kleenex beside my chair, and the medical degrees on her wall.

"Well…he'd been after Mom and me since we ran away," I say at last. I finger the tiny cracks in the leather of the right armrest. Then, bit by bit, I start telling her, including random stuff I'd forgotten until I hear myself saying it. Before I know it, the words are a flood. I can't stop, but I have to—the hour is over.

I'm seeing her tomorrow and the next day, and then twice a week for as long as I need.

"How was it?" Mom asks when I get back in the car.

"Fine."

"What all did you talk about?"

"Not much." I smile. "Nothing about you, if that's what you mean."

Mom blushes. "Sorry. I shouldn't have asked."

All the way back to the farm, I look at the fields and think about the session. Today all I talked about was Dad. Pretty soon though, I'd like to talk about Jacky. The coroner's report has just come out. Like we figured, he died of suffocation. The coroner said his bones had five healed fractures.

Jacky.

I love Mom, but there are things I think I could say to Dr. Harrison that I'd never be able say to *her*. At least not yet.

Mr. Sinclair drops by midevening. He's been in a great mood since seeing about the farm, but tonight he's clicking his tongue more than normal. "I've just come from a meeting of the town council. They've agreed that Jacky can be reburied in the clearing."

"That's fantastic."

"A couple of councilors squawked how they didn't like burials on private land, but I argued that the township has no laws against it.

Besides, Jacky'd already been there thirty years, and the clearing is out of sight and mind. So in the end they decided to leave things be."

"Jacky would be so happy."

Mr. Sinclair nods. "Something else that would make him happy too: the council gave permission for his mother to be buried beside him. All things considered, it's only right—the two of them together, resting peacefully forever."

Mom asks Mr. Sinclair to sit down and brings out some food. "We have some news too. Would you like to tell him, Cameron?"

"You bet." And I do.

My news is the best news ever, even if it's not really a surprise.

I mean, I've always kind of known that Mom watches me when I'm smiling at Ken. A couple of times she's said, "You and Ken seem to be getting along better than in the beginning."

When she fishes like that, I roll my eyes, sigh, and say, "Mom," or "Sure, why not?" because, come on, who talks about stuff like that? But it's true and she knows it. I've teased them about how *they're* getting on too: "Are you guys going to get married?" Which makes Ken grin and Mom flick her napkin at me. "I've had one marriage too many, don't you think?"

All the same, we all know Ken wouldn't still be here or have ever stayed in her room if they weren't serious. So this morning at breakfast, when they asked if I'd mind us moving into Ken's place, I was more than ready.

"Mind? I've been packed for weeks."

I still don't know if Mom and Ken will ever get married. What I do know is, whatever they decide, from now on we're a family. I hear them talk about our future all the time. It makes me happier than I ever thought was possible.

Ken's a great guy. I never knew what a real dad was before. I do now. A real dad is someone who loves your mom and treats her right, and cares about you more than anything.

My bags are packed and ready to go. I'm in the clearing. There's a carpet of fresh crisp snow halfway up my boots.

"I'm leaving," I tell Jacky. "I've come to say good-bye."

If this was a story, I'd say that the sun comes out from behind a cloud—Jacky's way of saying he's happy for me. But I know Jacky's happy without that. His spirit is smiling inside me. Next time the wind is up and I hear the dogs, I won't be scared. They won't hurt me. He won't let them.

# Acknowledgments

Special thanks to Graham Mahood and Roger Gallibois for advice on wills and real estate; my editors Charlie Sheppard and Diane Kerner for some of the best notes ever; and Daniel Legault, Louise and Christine Baldacchino, Vickie Stewart, Alan King, Susan Izumi, and Elva Mai Hoover for being *The Dogs*'s first eyes and ears.

# About the Author

Allan Stratton is the internationally acclaimed author of the Michael L. Printz Honor Book *Chanda's Secrets*: it was made into the award-winning Cannes Film Festival hit, *Life, Above All*. His novels *Leslie's Journal* and *Borderline* were American Library Association Best Books for Young Adults; *Chanda's Wars* and *The Grave Robber's Apprentice* were Junior Library Guild selections. His current novel, *The Dogs*, is being published in thirteen countries.

Allan has gone on photographic safaris in Africa, hiked the Great Wall of China, explored pyramids in Egypt, and flown over Cappadocia in a balloon. In addition to travel, he loves animals, especially his four cats, who sit on his lap and help him write. You can see a full list of Allan's awards as well as reviews, book trailers and video interviews, by visiting him at his website: www.allanstratton.com.